COMPLETE CHILDREN'S
COOKBOOK

DK | Penguin Random House

Project Editor Elizabeth Yeates
US Editor Margaret Parrish
Designer Vanessa Hamilton
Special Sales Creative Project Manager
Alison Donovan
Pre-Production Producer Dragana Puvacic
Producer Ché Creasey

First American Edition, 2015
Published in the United States by DK Publishing
345 Hudson Street, New York, New York 10014

A catalog record for this book
is available from the Library of Congress.
ISBN 978-1-4654-3546-0

DK books are available at special discounts when purchased
in bulk for sales promotions, premiums, fund-raising, or
educational use. For details, contact: DK Publishing Special
Markets, 345 Hudson Street, New York, New York 10014
SpecialSales@dk.com

Material in this publication was previously published in:
Children's Cookbook (2004), *Grow It, Cook It* (2008),
Cookbook for Girls (2009), *The Children's Baking Book* (2010),
How Does My Garden Grow? (2011), *How to Cook* (2011),
How Cooking Works (2012), *Cook It* (2013)

Printed and bound in China by Hung Hing

A WORLD OF IDEAS:
SEE ALL THERE IS TO KNOW

www.dk.com

COMPLETE CHILDREN'S
COOKBOOK

Contents

Before you begin

Breakfast

Soups and salads

Light bites

Main meals

Desserts

Cakes and muffins

Cookies and bars

Bread

Party time

BEFORE YOU BEGIN

Healthy eating

You need to eat a balanced diet made up of a variety of different foods, so that you can grow, stay healthy, and have lots of energy for life.

Fruits and vegetables

Your body can get important vitamins and minerals, as well as fiber, from fruits and vegetables. Aim to eat about five different portions of these a day. It's useful to think of a portion as roughly equal to the amount you can hold in one hand—such as an apple, a small bunch of grapes, two broccoli florets, or a bowl of salad.

Starchy foods

Bread, cereals, rice, pasta, and potatoes are all starchy foods, also known as carbohydrates. These foods give you energy and should form a part of every meal—whether it's cereal for breakfast, a sandwich at lunch, or a pasta dish for dinner. Many starchy foods come in whole-grain varieties, which are healthier for you since they contain more vitamins, minerals, and fiber, when compared with the refined white versions.

Protein

This type of food is made from amino acids, chemicals that work all over your body to keep you active and strong. We eat protein from both animal and plant sources—meat, fish, nuts, and seeds, beans, and dairy. It's healthy to eat a variety of these.

Dairy

In addition to being a source of protein, dairy provides valuable vitamins (vitamins A, B12, and D) and minerals (such as calcium). Dairy includes milk, yogurt, cheese, butter, cream, sour cream, and cottage cheese. If you're not fond of dairy, then you can get these nutrients in other foods, such as soy milk, tofu, and baked beans.

Fats and sugars

Everyone needs fat for energy and for their bodies to work properly, but it has to be the right type of fat. Fats also help you absorb vitamins and provide essential fatty acids, such as omega-3 and omega-6. Healthy fats (known as polyunsaturated or monounsaturated) are found in vegetable oils, such as sesame, sunflower, soy, and olive, as well as in nuts, seeds, avocados, and oily fish, such as mackerel and salmon. Avoid eating saturated and trans fats (mostly in processed foods).

Sugary foods and salt

Sugar gives you energy and it makes cookies and cakes taste sweet. Eating too much sugar, though, can lead to mood swings, tooth decay, and obesity. Too much salt is linked with health problems. Avoid very salty snacks and don't add too much salt to your cooking.

weights and measurements

Use measuring cups and spoons, a liquid measuring cup, and weighing scales, as necessary. Measure ingredients before you start a recipe. Below are the full names for measurements and their abbreviations.

Metric measures

g = gram

ml = milliliter

US measures

oz = ounce

lb = pound

fl oz = fluid ounce

Spoon measures

tsp = teaspoon

tbsp = tablespoon

Cook's notes

• Gather and prepare all ingredients before you start cooking—you don't want to discover halfway through a recipe that you have run out of something important.

• All fruits and vegetables listed in recipes are medium sized unless otherwise stated.

• Use medium-sized eggs unless otherwise stated, and free-range if possible.

• Always use the type of flour specified in a recipe—bread, all-purpose, or self-rising.

• It's important to preheat the oven for 10 minutes or so before using it so the correct temperature is reached.

• Preparation and cooking times are only a guide. Cooking times may vary according to the type of pan, or oven, and the ripeness of ingredients.

• The easiest way to make cooking stock is using a bouillon cube or powder and adding the correct quantity of water, according to instructions on the package.

Kitchen hygiene

When you're in the kitchen, follow these important rules to keep the germs in check.

• Always wash your hands before you start.

• Wash all fruits and vegetables.

• Any cutting board or knife used in the preparation of raw poultry, meat, or fish should be cleaned thoroughly with hot soapy water before using it again.

• Raw eggs carry a risk of contamination from the salmonella bacterium. Do not give foods with uncooked eggs in them to babies and young children, pregnant women, or the elderly.

• Use separate cutting boards for meat and vegetables.

• Always check the use-by dates on ingredients, and don't use them if the date has passed.

Safety

• Always use oven mitts when handling hot pans and baking sheets.

• Don't put hot pans directly on to the work surface, but use a hot pad, metal rack or trivet, or wooden or heatproof board.

• A sharp knife is safer than a blunt one, but remember that sharp knives should be used carefully and treated with respect.

• Wear an apron to protect your clothes.

• Keep the cooking area clean, and wipe up any spills that could cause accidents.

Equipment

Here is a handy guide for the equipment used in this book.
Each recipe has a tools checklist so that you can gather everything
you need before you begin cooking.

Whisk

Kitchen scissors

Pizza cutter

Fork

Peelers

Garlic crusher

Wooden Spoons

Basting brush

Large Spoon

Sharp knife

Butter knife

Spoons

Grater

Baking pans

Loaf pan

Nonstick muffin pan

Pizza pan

Cutting boards

Cooling rack

Plastic container

Small bowls

Large bowl

Colander

Glass bowls

Wok

Small saucepan

Food processor

Cutting board

Piping bag

Glass jar

Masher

Electric mixer

Food blender

Spatula

Plastic spatula

Ladle

Skewers

Sieve

Measuring Spoons

Egg cup

Slotted Spoon

Spaghetti claw

Ice cream scoop

Measuring cup

Pastry cutter

Ramekin

Lemon juicer

Cookie cutters

Round cake pan

Glass pitchers

Rolling pin

Parchment paper

Square cake pan

Foil

Baking dish

Ceramic flan dish

Lasagne dish

Metal pie plate

Plastic wrap

Stock pot

Frying pan

Small Dutch oven

Saucepan with lid

Grill pan

Ways to cook

Some foods are best cooked at low heat for a long time, while others respond best to a fast blast of heat. The different techniques shown below are used in different recipes to bring out the best flavors and textures of a dish.

Boil

With the heat turned up high, a liquid will bubble vigorously when boiling.

Simmer

With the heat on low, a mixture will bubble gently when simmering.

Fry

Drizzle some oil into a wide pan to fry food; it's also known as sautéing.

Stir-fry

On high heat and using oil, stir-frying cooks fast and needs lots of stirring.

Broil

With the heat coming from above, you need to turn food during broiling.

Griddle

On high heat, using a griddle or grill pan let's you grill food indoors.

Bake

Cooking food in an oven at low heat is baking. Bread, cakes, and pies are baked.

Roast

Cooking meat, fish, or vegetables in the oven at high heat is roasting.

Steam

Placing food above boiling water uses the steam to cook it.

Poach

Cooking in a simmering liquid, such as water or milk, is called poaching.

Deep-fry

Completely immersing food in hot oil is known as deep-frying.

Grill

Food can be grilled on a charcoal or gas grill outside.

Preparing ingredients

Before you start cooking you'll need to get all your ingredients ready. Depending on your recipe, you may have a lot of prep work or very little to do.

Dice

To dice an onion, first slice it (while keeping it together) and then slice it at right angles to create small squares or dice. For a zucchini, first cut into chunky sticks and then cut across these to make dice.

Chop

Claw Hold the food using a "claw" shape to keep fingers clear of the knife.

Bridge Form a bridge between thumb and finger and cut beneath the bridge.

Peel

Whatever you're peeling, hold the food in one hand and peel away from your body. Carrots are easily peeled from top to bottom but apples can be peeled in one beautiful spiral—with practice. And watch out for your fingers—peelers are sharp.

Grate

As the food passes over the grater's teeth, slivers are forced through.

Mash

Cooked root vegetables can be pushed through a masher until smooth.

Make bread crumbs

Before

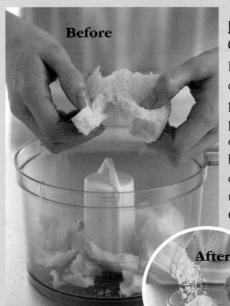

After

It's quickest done in a food processor. Tear pieces of dried-out bread into the bowl, pop the lid on, and pulse until crumbs form. Or, grate chunks of the bread instead.

15

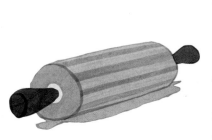

Ways to bake

To get cakes to rise, make light meringue, and perfect your pastry and cookies, there are certain techniques in baking that you'll need to master. Once you know what's what you'll be a baking expert!

Sift

Sifting confectioners' sugar and flour gets rid of lumps and adds air.

Fold

1. Use a spatula to mix gently while keeping the air in the mixture.

2. Go around the edge of the bowl and then "cut" across, lifting as you go.

Beat

Make a smooth, airy mixture by working fast with a wooden spoon.

Separate an egg

1. Break the shell: tap the egg on the side of the bowl and open up.

2. Transfer the yolk from one shell to the other; put the yolk in another bowl.

Whisk egg whites

1. Add lots of air into a mixture using an electric mixer or a handheld whisk.

2. The mixture should be stiff; if you overbeat the mixture it will collapse.

Rub in

1. Many recipes mix fat (diced butter) and flour using this method.

2. Using your fingertips, pick up the mixture, break up the lumps, and let it fall.

3. Keep rubbing your thumb along your fingertips. To check that you've gotten rid of the lumps of butter, shake the bowl and any lumps will pop to the surface.

Make a piping bag

1. Cut a square of wax paper or parchment paper.
2. Fold the paper around on itself to form a cone with a pointed end. Tape in place.

3. Snip off the end of the cone for the icing or frosting to come out: for a fine line, use a tiny cut; cut higher up the cone for a chunky line.

Cream

1. When mixing butter and sugar together, use butter that's been left to soften at room temperature.
2. Cut the butter into pieces.

3. Using an electric mixer or a wooden spoon, beat the butter and sugar together until the mixture is pale in color, light, and fluffy.

Knead

1. Use the heel of your hand to push the bread dough away from you.

2. Fold the squashed end of dough over and turn everything around.

3. Repeat the squashing, folding, and turning motions until the dough is silky soft and smooth. Now the dough is ready to proof.

Roll out

On a floured surface, push down on a rolling pin to make a large flat piece.

Grease a pan

Use parchment paper to spread a thin layer of butter all over the pan.

Line a pan

1. Draw around your pan and add some extra for the paper to go up the sides.

2. Position the paper in the pan. Fold at the corners; snip off extra bits.

Cooking rules

All recipes should be made under adult supervision. Cooking is lots of fun, but there are certain rules that you need to know before you begin.

Key to symbols used in the recipes

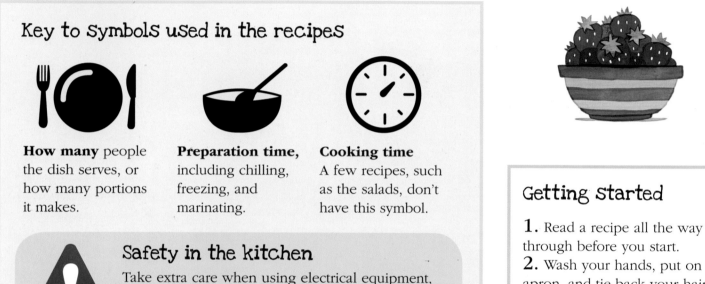

How many people the dish serves, or how many portions it makes.

Preparation time, including chilling, freezing, and marinating.

Cooking time A few recipes, such as the salads, don't have this symbol.

Safety in the kitchen
Take extra care when using electrical equipment, and when this symbol appears, as hot ovens or sharp implements are used.

Getting started

1. Read a recipe all the way through before you start.
2. Wash your hands, put on an apron, and tie back your hair.
3. Make sure you have all the ingredients and equipment before you begin a recipe.

Other useful terms

- **Toast** to make a food, such as bread or nuts, crisp, hot, and brown.
- **Purée** a thick pulp of vegetables or fruit blended until smooth.
- **Marinate** to mix food with a combination of oil, wine, or vinegar with herbs or spices to add flavor.

- **Blend** to mix together so you can't see any of the individual ingredients.
- **Punch down** bash the excess air out when bread dough has risen, before letting it proof.
- **Drizzle** to pour a little stream of liquid, such as olive oil, in tiny drops.
- **Season** to add salt and pepper.
- **Toss** mix some dry ingredients in some wet ingredients, such as lettuce

leaves in salad dressing or pasta shapes in a sauce.
- **Reduce to thicken** heating a sauce gently until some of its water is lost (as steam) and the amount of sauce becomes less.
- **Baste** to coat food with meat juice, a marinade or butter, while cooking.

Estimated preparation and cooking times help you to plan your meals.

The ingredients are pictured to help you find them, but remember, they do not show the exact quantities!

Step-by-step pictures and explanations help you to follow the recipes.

Variation and tip boxes suggest different ingredients you can use in the dish and how to ensure it tastes perfect.

Mini burgers

These mini burgers are hard to beat. Make them for your family and friends. They'll soon be asking you when you're going to serve them again!

30 mins 15 mins Serves 6

Ingredients
- 9oz (250g) ground beef
- 1¾ oz (50g) Parmesan cheese, freshly grated
- ¼ cup fresh bread crumbs
- 1½ tbsp olive oil
- ½ garlic clove, crushed
- 1 tbsp onion, finely chopped
- 1 egg
- 1 tsp dried oregano
- olive oil, for frying

To Serve
- 16 mini hamburger buns
- 2 tomatoes, thinly sliced
- lettuce leaves
- 14 oz (400g) jar tomato sauce or salsa

Equipment
- large mixing bowl
- baking sheet
- frying pan
- spatula
- bread knife

1 Combine all the ingredients for the burgers in a bowl. Use your hands to mix everything together.

2 Form the mixture into balls and then flatten them. Chill the burgers in the fridge for 30 minutes. Wash your hands well.

3 Fry the burgers over medium heat. Make sure the meat is cooked through by putting a fork in and checking that the juice runs clear.

4 Carefully cut the buns in half. Fill each bun with a cooked hamburger, a tomato slice, a lettuce leaf, and tomato sauce.

Tip
You can decorate your mini burgers before serving them. Make flags out of colored strips of paper.

284

285

A tools checklist helps you to gather everything that you need before you start cooking.

This symbol warns you to take extra care because the step involves heat or sharp objects.

A colorful picture gives you an idea on how to serve the dish.

BREAKFAST

Fruit smoothie

Smoothies are easy to make and taste delicious at any time of day. Follow these four simple steps for a burst of fruity goodness.

10 mins   Serves 2-4

Ingredients

- 1 ripe banana
- 7oz (200g) ripe strawberries
- ¾ cup milk
- 1tbsp honey
- ½ cup plain yogurt

Equipment

- sharp knife
- cutting board
- measuring spoons
- blender

1

Rinse and drain the strawberries in cold water and then hull them by holding the pointed end and slicing off the stem.

2

Cut the strawberries in half and put them to one side. Peel the banana and throw away the peel. Slice the banana so it blends easily in step 4.

3

Carefully put the banana and strawberries into the blender. Add the milk, yogurt, and honey, then put the lid on securely.

4

Blend the mixture until it is completely smooth. Pour the smoothie into tall glasses and enjoy—what a great way to start the day!

24

Grilled fruit and honey

You will love this fruit grilled—it helps bring out the sweetness. If you don't have a grill pan, place the fruit under a hot broiler.

1

Cut each peach in half and remove the pit. Then cut each into quarters. Halve the apricots and remove the pits.

2

In a large bowl, mix together the sugar and cinnamon, then add the fruit. Toss to coat in the sugar mixture.

3

Preheat a grill pan and add the peaches, flesh side down. Cook for 2 to 3 minutes. Add the apricots, and turn over the peaches. Cook until caramelized.

4

Meanwhile, place the yogurt in a bowl and pour in the honey. Stir to create a rippled effect. Serve the warmed grilled fruit with the yogurt and honey dip.

10 mins   6 mins   Serves 4

Ingredients

- 3 peaches
- 4 apricots
- 2 tbsp sugar
- $\frac{1}{2}$ tsp ground cinnamon
- 1 cup Greek yogurt
- 2 tbsp honey

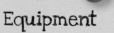

Equipment

- knife
- cutting board
- 2 mixing bowls
- 2 metal spoons
- grill pan
- tongs

Fruity granola

Ingredients

- 2 tbsp sunflower oil
- 6 tbsp maple syrup or honey
- 3¾ cups rolled oats
- 1 cup hazelnuts
- ½ cup pumpkin seeds
- 1 cup dried banana chips, broken into small pieces
- ¾ cup raisins
- milk or plain yogurt to serve

Equipment

- large saucepan
- wooden spoon
- large bowl
- baking sheet
- oven mitts
- airtight container to store granola in afterward

You need a hearty breakfast to keep you going through the morning. This delicious granola will keep you filled up until snack time. If you like, you can use dried cranberries instead of raisins.

Ask an adult to preheat the oven to 400°F (200°C). Heat the oil and maple syrup or honey in a saucepan over low heat.

Pour the maple syrup and oil mixture into a large bowl with the oats, hazelnuts, and pumpkin seeds.

Place the mixture onto a baking sheet, spread it out, and cook in the oven for 10 minutes, or until the granola turns a golden brown color.

Let the oat mixture cool on the sheet and then pour it into a bowl. Add the dried banana chips and raisins to the mixture and stir well.

5 **Serve your granola** in a bowl with milk or a spoonful of plain yogurt.

Sticky stuff

The sugar and maple syrup act like a glue in this recipe. They help the dry ingredients stick together, making the granola bars incredibly chewy and sticky!

Granola bars

Granola bars are perfect for breakfast or as a snack. Once you've mastered this recipe, experiment with other fruits and nuts.

15 mins   30 mins   Serves 12

Ingredients

- 8 tbsp unsalted butter
- ½ cup light brown sugar
- ½ cup maple syrup or honey
- 3 cups rolled oats
- ¾ cup raisins
- ½ cup mixed nuts, chopped

Equipment

- 12 x 9 x 1½in (30 x 23 x 4cm) baking pan
- parchment paper
- wooden spoon
- saucepan

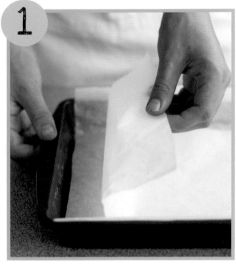

1

Preheat the oven to 300°F (150°C). Grease your baking pan, then line it with 2 sheets of parchment paper.

2

Melt the butter, sugar, and maple syrup (or honey) in a saucepan over low heat.

3

Place all the other ingredients in a large bowl and pour in the sugar mixture.

4

Spread the mixture evenly in the baking pan and, using a masher, press it down firmly so it sticks together. Bake for 20–30 minutes, or until golden brown.

5

When the granola bars are baked, let them cool for 5 minutes. Then, using a cloth to hold the pan, cut them into 12 squares. Remove them from the pan when fully cooled and firm.

French toast

Popular around the world, this dish is eaten in Portugal at Christmas and in Spain and Brazil at Easter.

10 mins   10 mins   Serves 2

Ingredients

- 4 large eggs
- 1 cup milk
- ¼ tsp ground cinnamon
- 4 slices thick white bread, cut into triangles
- 2 tbsp sunflower oil
- 3½oz (100g) blueberries
- maple syrup, to serve

Equipment

- whisk
- mixing bowl
- shallow dish
- frying pan and spatula

1

Crack the eggs into a mixing bowl. Add the milk and cinnamon and whisk together.

2

Pour the mixture into a shallow dish. Soak the bread in the mixture for about 30 seconds.

3

Heat half a tablespoon of the oil in a frying pan on low heat. Carefully place two triangles in the pan.

4

Fry the triangles on both sides until they turn golden brown. Repeat steps 3 and 4 for the remaining bread triangles.

5

Serve the French toast warm, with blueberries and maple syrup or try it with butter and jam.

Four ways with eggs

Eggs are perfect for breakfast, and they're packed with goodness to start your day. You can cook eggs in different ways to vary your breakfast.

1

Scrambled eggs with bacon

The secret to scrambled eggs is not to overcook them, otherwise they become dry and rubbery.

Ingredients

This recipe is for 1 person. It takes 2 minutes to prepare and 8 minutes to cook.

- 1 strip bacon
- 1 tbsp milk
- 1 egg
- 1 small pat butter
- pinch of dried basil
- 1 slice buttered toast

Method

- Ask an adult to fry the bacon. When it's cooked, use a knife and fork to cut it into small pieces.

- Whisk together the milk and egg until creamy.

- Melt the butter in a frying pan on medium heat and add the egg and milk mixture. Stir often, until the eggs are just cooked but still creamy. Mix in the fried bacon pieces.

2

Boiled eggs

How do you like your egg boiled? Look at the options below and decide how long to cook your egg.

Ingredients

This recipe is for 1 person. It takes 2 minutes to prepare and 4–8 minutes to cook.

- 1 egg
- 1 slice buttered toast, cut into strips

Method

- Fill a small saucepan with water and lower one egg into it. Ask an adult to boil the water. When the water has boiled, lower the temperature and let it simmer.

- SOFT-BOILED
Cook for four minutes. This egg will have a soft, runny yolk—perfect if you like to dip your slices of toast!

- MEDIUM-BOILED
Cook for six minutes. The egg yolk will be medium-firm.

- HARD-BOILED
Cook for eight minutes. The yolk will be very firm.

Make your own

The eggs of many different types of bird can be eaten, but those of the female chicken (hens) are the most common and are widely available.

Quail

Duck

Hen

Gull

Goose

Ostrich

3

Fried eggs

If you like your egg yolk runny, then fry the egg on one side only. If you prefer them well-done, fry on both sides.

Ingredients

This recipe is for 1 person. It takes 1 minute to prepare and 2–4 minutes to cook.

· 1 tsp sunflower oil

· 1 egg

· 1 slice buttered toast

· ground black pepper, to season

Method

• Ask an adult to heat the oil in a pan over medium heat.

• Crack the egg into a bowl. If any of the shell falls into the bowl scoop it out using a spoon. Gently pour the egg into the frying pan.

• The egg needs to be fried for about two minutes on medium heat. If you like your eggs well-done, carefully flip the egg with a spatula.

• Serve the fried egg on a slice of toast. Season with black pepper.

4

Poached eggs

Poaching eggs can be tricky, but keep practicing and you will soon master the technique to create a perfect poached egg.

Ingredients

This recipe is for 1 person. It takes 5 minutes to prepare and 2–4 minutes to cook.

· 1 egg

· 1 slice buttered toast

Method

• Fill a large saucepan with water and ask an adult to boil the water. When the water has boiled, lower the temperature so the water is barely boiling.

• Crack the egg into a cup and carefully pour it into the water.

• The egg needs to be poached for about 2 minutes, or until the white is set.

• Carefully remove the egg with a slotted spoon and place it on a piece of paper towel to drain.

• Serve on a slice of buttered toast.

Potato rösti

This classic Swiss dish is made from grated potatoes that are fried until crispy. You can make big pan-sized röstis, but these smaller ones are easier to turn. Eat them for breakfast or as a side dish to a main meal.

20 mins | 10–20 mins | Makes 8

Ingredients

• 3–4 medium-sized russet potatoes, about 2lb (900g), peeled

• salt and freshly ground black pepper

• 4 tbsp olive oil

Equipment

• saucepan
• colander
• grater
• bowl
• clean dish towel
• fork
• large frying pan
• metal spoon
• spatula

1

Cut the potatoes in half and parboil them in a saucepan of boiling salted water for 6–7 minutes. Drain and let cool.

2

Coarsely grate the potatoes into a bowl or onto a plate—graters with big holes are best. Transfer the potatoes to a clean dish towel.

3

Use the dish towel to squeeze out any excess liquid, which would make the rösti soggy. Add the salt and pepper, and mix lightly with a fork.

4

Heat half the oil in a large frying pan and let it begin to sizzle. Shape spoonfuls of the grated potato mixture into round cakes ½–¾in (1–2cm) thick and place four of them into the pan.

34

5

Gently fry the rösti

for about 5–10 minutes, or until golden brown and crisp underneath. Turn them with a spatula, then cook for another 5–10 minutes, or until browned on the other side. Remove from the pan and keep warm while cooking the rest of the mixture in the remaining oil.

Variation

Get inventive and mix the potato with other delicious root vegetables, such as sweet potatoes, carrots, parsnips, or even beets.

Breakfast omelet

This omelet is a tasty variation of the traditional breakfast. It has all the right ingredients for a filling weekend brunch—eggs, bacon, tomato, mushrooms—and can even be served with a mixed salad as a light or main meal.

10 mins   15 mins   Serves 1

Ingredients

- 2 eggs
- 2 tbsp milk
- 1oz (30g) cheddar cheese
- 1 pat unsalted butter
- salt and pepper

For the filling

- 1 tomato
- 2 strips bacon
- 1 tsp sunflower oil
- 2oz (60g) mushrooms

Equipment

- whisk
- liquid measuring cup
- grater
- wooden spoon
- sharp knife
- 2 cutting boards
- small nonstick frying pan or omelet pan
- wooden spatula
- 2 plates
- paper towels

Whisk the eggs and milk together in a liquid measuring cup. (This will make it easy to pour in step 5.) Grate the cheese and stir it into the egg mixture. Season.

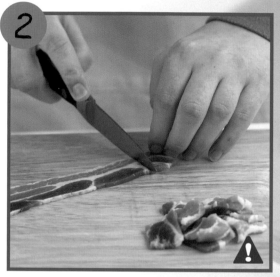

Cut the tomato into chunks and slice the mushrooms. On a separate cutting board, cut the bacon into cubes.

Place the frying pan over medium heat and fry the bacon for 3 minutes, or until cooked completely. Put the bacon on a plate lined with paper towels.

Heat the oil and fry the mushrooms for 2 minutes. Add the tomato to the pan and cook for 1 minute. Put the tomato and mushrooms onto a plate.

Melt the butter in the pan. Pour in the eggs so they cover the bottom of the pan. Cook the eggs on medium heat until the edges begin to cook and set.

Using a spatula, push the cooked egg into the center of the pan. The uncooked egg will run to the sides. Repeat until all the egg is cooked.

Shake the pan to release the omelet and spoon the filling over one half. Slide the omelet out onto a plate and gently flip the unfilled half over the top.

Pancakes

Ingredients

- 1 egg
- ²⁄₃ cup self-rising flour
- 1 tsp baking soda
- ²⁄₃ cup milk
- sunflower oil for frying
- 7oz (200g) fresh strawberries
- 4 tbsp plain yogurt

Equipment

- mixing bowl
- liquid measuring cup
- whisk
- frying pan
- tablespoon
- spatula

Pancakes can be thick or thin depending on the ingredients you use to make them. Have fun trying out both types of pancake. Thin pancakes are often called "crêpes." Make this dish for your family.

Wash the strawberries and cut a few of them into halves and place to one side (they will be used for decoration). Hull the remaining strawberries and carefully cut into slices.

Put the egg, flour, baking soda, and milk into a bowl. Whisk the mixture until it's smooth.

Heat a tablespoon of sunflower oil in a frying pan. Use a large spoon to pour the pancake mixture into the pan carefully. Fry the pancake until golden brown on the bottom.

Flip the pancake and fry the other side. Place a few strawberry slices and a tablespoon of yogurt on a pancake, then a pancake on top. Repeat until you have a two layers of strawberries.

Tip

Put half the muffins in an airtight container and place in the freezer to have at a later date. The muffins can stay in the freezer for up to two months.

Blueberry muffins

Muffins are delicious for breakfast or dessert. The blueberries make the muffins extra moist and yummy. They pop while they cook to create great bursts of color.

Preheat the oven to 400°F (200°C). Line a 12-cup muffin pan with paper liners. Melt the butter in a pan, then set aside to cool. Sift the flour into a bowl, and mix in the baking powder, sugar, and lemon zest.

Make a well in the center of the flour. Mix the yogurt, eggs, and cooled melted butter together in a large pitcher, then pour into the dry ingredients.

Add the blueberries. Mix until just combined, but don't overmix or the muffins will be heavy.

Spoon evenly into the paper liners and bake for 20 minutes, or until golden brown and springy. Cool in the pan for 5 minutes.

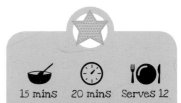

15 mins   20 mins   Serves 12

Ingredients

- 4 tbsp unsalted butter
- 2 cups self-rising flour
- 1 tsp baking powder
- ¼ cup superfine sugar
- finely grated zest of 1 lemon (optional)
- 1 cup plain yogurt
- 2 large eggs, lightly beaten
- 9oz (250g) blueberries

Equipment

- mixing bowl
- sieve
- large pitcher
- wooden spoon
- 2 soup spoons
- 12-cup muffin pan and paper liners

Ingredients

- 2 cups all-purpose flour
- 1 tbsp baking powder
- ¾ cup rolled oats
- ¾ cup dried apricots (chopped)
- ⅓ cup light brown sugar
- ½ tsp salt
- 2 eggs, beaten
- ⅔ cup milk
- ⅓ cup sunflower oil
- 5 tbsp honey

Equipment

- 2 x 6-hole or 12-hole muffin pan
- 10 paper paper liners
- large mixing bowl
- sieve
- wooden spoon
- liquid measuring cup
- fork
- oven mitts
- cooling rack

Oat and honey muffins

These light and fluffy muffins are perfect for breakfast or a midmorning snack because they are packed with nutritious oats and dried fruit.

Preheat the oven to 375°F (190°C). Line a muffin pan with 10 paper cases. Sift the flour and baking powder into a bowl and stir in the oats, apricots, sugar, and salt.

Put the flour mixture to one side. In a large measuring cup, mix the eggs, milk, oil, and honey with a fork until thoroughly combined and frothy.

Pour the wet mixture in the measuring cup over the dry ingredients in the bowl. Stir with a wooden spoon until the ingredients are just combined. The batter will be lumpy and runny.

Divide the mixture between the paper liners so they are two-thirds full. Cook on the top shelf of the oven for 20–25 minutes. Leave in the pan for a few minutes, then transfer to a cooling rack.

Variation

Don't like apricots? Just replace them with your favorite dried fruit, such as papaya or mango.

SOUPS AND SALADS

Tomato soup

Soup is a comforting meal or snack and it makes an easy appetizer to a main meal. This soup is wonderfully thick and creamy and is topped with small pieces of toast, called croutons.

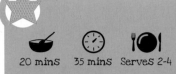

20 minS   35 minS   Serves 2-4

Ingredients

- 1 small onion
- 1 small carrot
- 4 tbsp olive oil
- 1 garlic clove, crushed
- 1 tbsp all-purpose flour
- 14oz (400g) can chopped tomatoes
- 1 tbsp tomato paste
- 1 tsp fresh thyme leaves (optional)
- 2 cups vegetable stock
- a pinch of sugar
- a squeeze of lemon juice
- 2 thick slices of bread
- salt and pepper

Equipment

- sharp knife
- peeler
- cutting board
- medium saucepan
- wooden spatula
- cookie cutters
- bread knife
- nonstick baking sheet
- oven mitts
- ladle
- blender

1

Peel and chop the onion and carrot. Ask an adult to preheat the oven to 425°F (220°C). Heat half the olive oil in the saucepan over medium heat.

2

Add the onion and carrot and cook for about 5 minutes to soften, stirring occasionally. Stir in the garlic and flour and cook the mixture for 1 minute.

3

Add the tomatoes, paste, thyme, stock, sugar, and lemon juice and bring to a boil. Reduce the heat and simmer for 20–25 minutes. Remove from the heat and cool.

4

While the soup is cooking, use cookie cutters to cut out shapes for the croutons. Scatter the bread on the baking sheet, drizzle over the remaining olive oil.

5

Use your hands to coat the bread in the oil and season. Bake for 8–10 minutes, until crisp and golden. Turn after about 4 minutes for even cooking.

6

Ladle the cool soup into the blender and blend until smooth. Reheat in a saucepan, then ladle into bowls. Serve with the croutons on top.

Butternut Squash soup

This wholesome, warming soup is perfect for a cold day. It's made from roasted butternut squash, but you can use pumpkin instead if you prefer.

15 mins   40 mins   Serves 4

Ingredients

- 2lb (1kg) butternut squash
- 1 tbsp vegetable oil
- 1 onion, chopped
- 2 cups hot vegetable stock
- 2 tbsp honey

To serve
- baguette
- Gruyére or Swiss cheese
- freshly chopped parsley

Equipment
- tablespoon
- vegetable peeler
- baking sheet
- wooden spoon
- food processor
- large saucepan

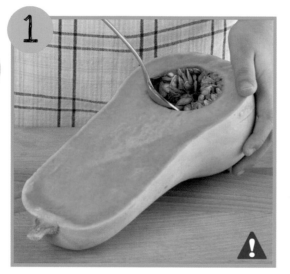

Preheat the oven to 400°F (200°C). Cut the butternut squash in half lengthwise, then use a spoon to scoop out the seeds and pith.

Cut into large chunks, then, using a peeler, remove the skin. Cut the chunks into 1in (2.5cm) cubes.

Place on a baking sheet, season with salt and pepper, then drizzle the oil on top. Roast for 20 minutes; remove from the oven.

Add the onion and stir. Return to the oven and cook for another 15 minutes. Remove from the oven and let cool a little.

Place the butternut squash and onion in a food processor with half of the stock Blend until smooth.

6

Place the paste in a saucepan with the remaining stock and honey. Simmer for 3 to 4 minutes. Serve with slices of toasted baguette, cheese, and parsley.

Pea and mint soup

This soup can be eaten hot or cold, so you can have it all year round! For a different flavor, add bacon and crème fraiche. Serve with fresh, crusty bread.

10 mins 5 mins Serves 4

Ingredients

- 9oz (250g) frozen peas, such as petit pois
- 2 cups hot vegetable stock
- pinch of freshly grated nutmeg
- handful of fresh mint leaves, coarsely chopped, or 1 tbsp of dried mint
- a few fresh thyme stalks, leaves picked (optional)
- ground black pepper
- 4 slices crusty bread, to serve

Equipment

- tea kettle
- mixing bowl
- large plate
- large pitcher
- blender
- saucepan

Put the peas in a bowl, then pour in boiling water. Cover and let stand for about 5 minutes. Pour into a colander over a sink to drain off the water.

Using a blender, pulse the peas, stock, nutmeg, and herbs until smooth and combined. Add more stock if the soup is too thick. Season well with black pepper.

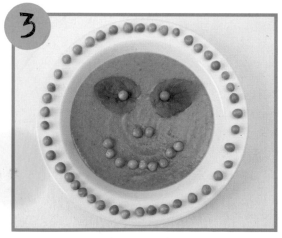

Spoon into cups or serve in a bowl. Have fun—make a face using fresh peas and mint leaves!

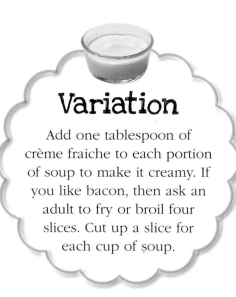

Variation

Add one tablespoon of crème fraiche to each portion of soup to make it creamy. If you like bacon, then ask an adult to fry or broil four slices. Cut up a slice for each cup of soup.

50

Onion and leek soup

Onions and leeks are great for adding flavor to savory meals. They also contain vitamins and minerals that will help keep your heart healthy.

Melt the butter in a large saucepan, then add the onion and leeks. Cook gently for about 5–7 minutes, until the onion and leeks are softened.

Add the potatoes and stock. Cook for another 10 minutes, or until the potatoes are tender.

Stir in the tarragon. Remove from the heat and let cool. It is dangerous to blend a soup when it is hot because the heat will force the lid off the blender.

Pour the cold mixture into a blender. Blend until smooth. Reheat with the milk in a saucepan to make soup. Season with salt and pepper.

10 mins   20 mins   Serves 4

Ingredients
- 4 tbsp butter
- 4 leeks, trimmed and sliced
- 1 large onion, chopped
- 2 medium potatoes, chopped
- 3½ cups chicken stock
- small bunch of tarragon, chopped
- 1 cup milk
- salt and pepper
- crème fraîche

Equipment
- cutting board
- sharp knife
- saucepan
- wooden spoon
- blender

Noodle soup

This is a healthy, filling, and complete meal in a bowl. Best of all, it only uses one saucepan, so there is not much to clean up afterward!

15-20 mins | 15 mins | Serves 2

Ingredients

- 2 tsp vegetable oil
- 2 scallions, trimmed and sliced diagonally
- 1 thin slice fresh ginger, peeled (optional)
- juice of ½ lime
- 2 cups fish stock (made with ⅓ of bouillon cube)
- 1 tsp soy sauce
- 2½ oz (75g) thin egg noodles
- 2oz (60g) baby corn, halved
- 2oz (60g) sugar snap peas
- 1 drop sesame oil
- 4oz (125g) ready-to-cook raw shrimp, shelled
- 2 tsp of chopped cilantro (optional)

Equipment

- medium saucepan
- wooden spoon
- liquid measuring cup

Heat the vegetable oil in a medium saucepan. Gently fry the scallions over medium heat for 1–2 minutes, or until soft.

Stir the ginger, stock, lime juice, and soy sauce into the scallion and bring to a boil. Lower the heat and simmer for 2–3 minutes.

Remove the ginger. Add the noodles and corn and bring to a boil. After 1½ minutes, add the sugar snap peas and cook for another 1½ minutes.

Lower the heat to bring the soup back to simmer. Stir in the shrimp and cook them for 2–3 minutes, or until pink. Stir in the sesame oil and cilantro.

Tip

Do not overcook the shrimp—if you do, the texture will be rubbery! If you are using frozen shrimp, make sure you defrost them completely before cooking them.

Soups can be as simple or as involved as you like. Enjoy them as an appetizer, or serve them with bread and turn them into a meal in themselves.

Pea soup

This vibrant soup is a perfect meal on a cold winter's day. Add cubes of fried bacon, or try the pea and mint soup recipe on pages 50–51.

Ingredients

This recipe is for 4 people. It takes 20 minutes to prepare and 15 minutes to cook.

- 4 scallions, sliced
- 4 tbsp butter
- 2 cups vegetable stock
- 12oz (350g) frozen peas
- 1/2 cup half-and-half
- 2 tsp chopped fresh mint

Method

- Cook the sliced scallions in the butter in a saucepan until soft.
- Add the vegetable stock and bring to a boil.
- Add the frozen peas, then simmer for 3–4 minutes. Cool for a few minutes.
- Pour into a blender and pulse until smooth.
- Return the soup to the saucepan and stir in the half-and-half and chopped fresh mint.
- Simmer gently for 5 minutes. Season with salt and freshly ground black pepper.

Hot tortilla soup

Add some grated cheese to melt into the soup when served. This will make the soup even more delicious. This recipe is for 4 people.

Ingredients

This soup takes 20 minutes to prepare and 20 minutes to cook.

- 1 onion
- 1 garlic clove
- 1 red chile
- 1 tbsp olive oil
- 1 tbsp paprika
- 3 1/2 cups tomato juice
- 1 1/4 cups vegetable stock
- 1/4 cup sunflower oil
- 2 soft corn tortillas
- 2 tbsp cilantro
- juice of 1 lime

Method

- Finely chop the onion, garlic, and chile and gently cook in the olive oil until soft.
- Add the paprika, tomato juice, and vegetable stock. Simmer for 15 minutes.
- Heat the sunflower oil in a frying pan, add strips of soft corn tortillas, and fry until crisp. Drain on paper towels.
- Stir in chopped cilantro and the lime juice, season with salt and freshly ground black pepper and top with the tortillas.

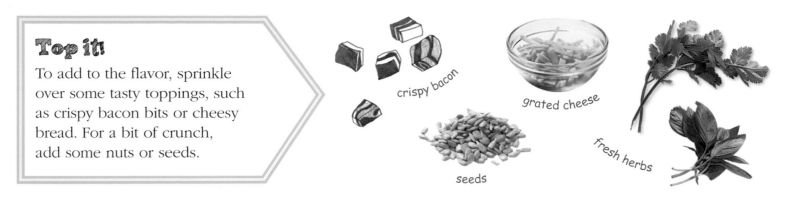

Top it!

To add to the flavor, sprinkle over some tasty toppings, such as crispy bacon bits or cheesy bread. For a bit of crunch, add some nuts or seeds.

crispy bacon

grated cheese

seeds

fresh herbs

3

Corn chowder

Chowder is a thick soup from New England. You can use fresh, frozen, or canned corn here.

Ingredients

This recipe is for 4 people. It takes 15 minutes to prepare and 30 minutes to cook.

· 1 large onion, chopped
· 9oz (200g) corn
· 1 large carrot, sliced
· 12oz (350g) potatoes, peeled and chopped
· 1 tbsp sunflower oil
· 1 bouquet garni (optional)
· 1 bay leaf
· 4 cups vegetable stock
· 1¼ cups milk

Method

• Gently cook the onion in the oil until soft.

• Add the corn, carrot, potatoes, bouquet garni, and bay leaf. Cook for 2 minutes, stirring constantly. Add the stock and bring to a boil.

• Reduce the heat to medium to low. Cover with a lid and cook for 15 minutes, stirring occasionally. Add the milk and cook for another 5 minutes.

• Scoop out some of the vegetables and blend the rest of the soup until smooth. Return the vegetables and blended soup to the pan and warm through.

4

Spicy lentil soup

This easy-to-make soup is really healthy. Serve it with cheesy croutons or crusty garlic bread.

Ingredients

This recipe is for 4 people. It takes 15 minutes to prepare and 35 minutes to cook.

· 2 onions
· 2 celery stalks
· 2 carrots
· 1 tbsp olive oil
· 2 finely chopped garlic cloves
· 1 tsp curry powder
· 5½oz (150g) red lentils
· 5 cups vegetable stock
· ½ cup tomato juice

Method

• Gently fry the onions, celery, and carrots—all finely chopped—in the olive oil.

• Cook for 5 minutes, then add the garlic and curry powder, and stir for another minute.

• Add the lentils, vegetable stock, and tomato juice. Bring to a boil, then reduce the heat. Cover, then simmer for 25 minutes.

• Season with salt and freshly ground black pepper and serve immediately.

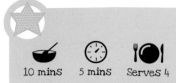

10 mins   5 mins   Serves 4

Ingredients

- 3½oz (100g) green beans, trimmed and halved
- 3½oz (100g) broccolini
- 3½oz (100g) fresh peas
- 5½oz (150g) mixed leaves, e.g., baby spinach, arugula, and watercress

Dressing

- 2 tbsp white wine vinegar
- 2 tbsp extra virgin olive oil
- 1 tbsp lemon juice
- 1 tsp honey
- 1 tsp pesto sauce

Equipment

- saucepan
- small mixing bowl
- whisk
- large serving bowl
- small pitcher

1

Place the green beans in a pan of boiling water for 2 minutes. Add the broccolini and peas. Simmer for 3 minutes, then drain.

2

Make the dressing. Place all the ingredients in a bowl, season with salt and a little freshly ground black pepper, then whisk until combined.

3

Put the salad leaves in a bowl and place the vegetables on top. Drizzle the dressing over the salad and toss together. Serve immediately.

Green salad

This salad makes a great accompaniment to grilled fish or chicken. You can add your own favorite vegetables—just remember to keep them green!

Tip

Once the vegetables are cooked, run them under cold water so they stop cooking and retain their color.

Variation

There are lots of other ingredients you can add to couscous. Include a handful of nuts or some cranberries. For a special treat, add pieces of grilled halloumi cheese.

Tomato and couscous salad

Salad makes a great light lunch, or it can be eaten as an appetizer. This super salad is full of interesting ingredients and looks pretty on the plate. It's tasty, too!

30 mins Serves 4

Ingredients
- 4 large tomatoes
- ²/₃ cup tomato juice
- ²/₃ cup couscous
- ²/₃ cup boiling water
- ¹/₃ cup raisins
- handful of basil leaves, chopped
- handful of flat-leaf parsley, torn (optional)

Equipment
- sharp knife
- cutting board
- teaspoon
- small glass bowl
- large glass bowl
- fork
- tablespoon

1

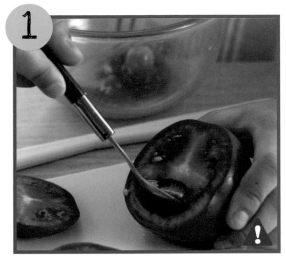

Slice off the tops of the tomatoes and scoop out the insides. Put the seeds and flesh into a bowl with the tomato juice.

2

Pour the boiling water over the couscous, cover, and let stand for 10 minutes. Use a fork to fluff up the grains. Add the tomato mixture and stir.

3

Add the raisins, basil, and parsley (if using), and mix. Taste, then season with ground black pepper as needed.

4

Spoon the mixture into the reserved tomato shells. Finally, serve with any leftover couscous mixture and garnish with lettuce leaves.

Tuna and bean salad

30 mins   Serves 4

Ingredients

- 4½ oz (125g) frozen fava beans
- 14oz (400g) can tuna in olive oil, drained
- 10 cherry tomatoes, halved
- handful of fresh chives, finely chopped
- ground black pepper
- 12 black olives, pitted
- 1 crisp head of lettuce, such as romaine, leaves separated
- 2-3 scallions, finely sliced

For the dressing

- 6 tbsp extra virgin olive oil
- 1 garlic clove, finely chopped
- 2 tbsp lemon juice
- 1-2 tsp Dijon mustard

Equipment

- large glass bowl
- colander
- screw-top jar
- 4 serving bowls

Salads are good for you and they help you get your five portions of fruit and vegetables a day. This salad is full of interesting ingredients and is fun to make.

1

Soak the fava beans in hot water for five minutes, then use a colander to drain. Set aside.

2

To make the dressing, put all the ingredients in a screw-top jar, season with black pepper, cover with the lid, and shake!

3

Put the tuna, tomatoes, and half of the dressing in a bowl. Sprinkle in half of the chives and season with the pepper. Gently mix in the beans and olives.

4

Spoon the tuna mixture on top of the lettuce. Drizzle with the remaining dressing, and sprinkle the scallions and remaining chives over the top.

62

Variation

If you don't like tuna, then substitute 14oz (400g) of cooked ham or cooked chicken pieces, shredded. Also, you can use green olives instead of black olives.

Rainbow salad

Food is full of color, and this healthy salad with a tofu dressing will bring dynamic color to the table. A serving bowl with blue in its pattern will complete the rainbow.

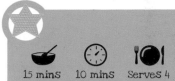

15 mins   10 mins   Serves 4

Ingredients

- mixed salad leaves
- 2 tbsp extra virgin olive oil
- 1 tbsp mustard seeds
- 9oz (250g) fresh peas
- ½ yellow, ½ orange bell pepper, cut into strips

- 12 cherry tomatoes, halved
- 2 carrots, cut into strips
- 2 raw beets, cut into strips
- 8 baby corn, cut in half lengthwise
- 1 tbsp sesame seeds
- 2 tbsp pumpkin seeds

Dressing

- 5oz (125g) silken tofu
- 2 tsp sesame oil

- ½ tbsp rice vinegar
- 1 tbsp soy sauce
- 1 tbsp extra virgin olive oil
- 1 tbsp honey
- 1 tbsp water
- mint, chopped
- salt and freshly ground black pepper

Croutons

- 6 slices whole wheat bread
- 2 tbsp extra virgin olive oil

Equipment

- coookie cutters
- baking sheet
- pastry brush
- blender
- colander
- colorful serving bowl
- sharp knife
- large frying pan

Cut shapes out of the bread, using cookie cutters. Brush the bread with olive oil and bake in the oven for about 5 minutes until golden brown.

Place all the ingredients for the dressing in a blender. Blend until smooth. Season with salt and pepper according to your taste.

Put the mixed leaves in a colander and wash. Drain well. Make a large bed of the leaves in a colorful serving bowl.

Heat the olive oil in a large frying pan and add the mustard seeds. Once they start to pop, add the beets, carrots, and baby corn. Cook them until just tender, then scatter on top of the salad ingredients in the bowl. Drizzle the dressing over the salad.

Scatter the pepper strips, fresh peas, and tomato halves on top of the salad leaves.

Ingredients

- 3 eggs
- 8oz (225g) small new potatoes, washed
- 4oz (115g) French beans, trimmed
- 6 small tomatoes, quartered
- 2 x 7oz (200g) cans tuna in olive oil, drained
- handful of fresh flat-leaf parsley, chopped
- bunch of fresh chives, finely chopped
- 12 black olives, pitted
- 2oz (50g) can anchovy fillets, drained
- 1 crisp head of lettuce, leaves separated and washed

For the dressing

- 6 tbsp olive oil
- 2 tbsp white wine vinegar
- 1 garlic clove, halved
- 2 tsp Dijon mustard
- salt and freshly ground black
- pepper

Equipment

- saucepan
- colander
- knife
- serving bowl
- screw-top jar

Salad niçoise

This is a great salad if you want something that's quick to make, filling, and really tasty. A specialty of the Côte d'Azur region of France and named after the city of Nice, Salad Niçoise is full of flavor, with salty anchovies and olives, juicy tuna, and fresh herbs.

1

Cook the eggs in a pan of simmering water for about 10 minutes. Cool in cold water and then remove the shells.

2

Boil the potatoes for about 10–15 minutes, or until tender when pierced with a knife. Drain and let cool, then cut in half, lengthwise. Simmer the French beans in a pan of water for 3 minutes, then drain and cool in cold water.

3

Put the potatoes, beans, tomatoes, tuna, herbs, olives, anchovies, and lettuce leaves in a large serving bowl.

4

Put all the dressing ingredients in a screw-top jar. Season well with salt and freshly ground black pepper. Make sure the lid is on tight, then shake well to combine all ingredients.

5

Remove the garlic from the dressing, then drizzle it over the salad and gently toss together. Quarter the eggs and arrange them on top. Serve with lots of fresh crusty bread to mop up the juices.

Variation

Add slices of Greek halloumi cheese cooked on a hot grill pan for 3 minutes on each side, or until it turns golden brown. Or use fresh mozzarella, torn into chunks, with a handful of fresh basil leaves.

Classic salads

These salads taste fantastic and healthy. Best of all, it won't take you long to prepare them. Try and use really fresh ingredients, which have more flavor.

1

Mozzarella, avocado, and tomato salad

Mozzarella, avocado, and tomato salad tastes delicious with fresh ciabatta bread.

Ingredients

This recipe is for 4 people. It takes 10 minutes to prepare.

• 6 tomatoes, sliced

• 2 peeled avocados

• 3 x 4½oz (125g) balls buffalo mozzarella

• fresh basil leaves

Method

• Slice the tomatoes, avocados, and buffalo mozzarella balls and layer onto a plate.

• Scatter the fresh basil leaves over the salad, followed by a sprinkling of salt and plenty of freshly ground black pepper.

• To serve, drizzle some extra virgin olive oil all over.

2

Greek salad

This fresh and vibrant salad is great on its own with a chunk of bread, but also tastes wonderful as a side dish with grilled meats.

Ingredients

This recipe is for 4 people. It takes 15 minutes to prepare.

• 4 tomatoes

• ½ cucumber, sliced

• ½ red onion, sliced

• 1 yellow bell pepper, sliced

• handful black olives

• lettuce leaves

• 5 oz (150g) diced feta cheese

• oregano leaves

• ¼ cup olive oil

• fresh lemon juice

Method

• Chop the tomatoes into wedges and mix in a bowl with the sliced cucumber, red onion, yellow bell pepper, and a handful of black olives.

• Pile on top of some lettuce leaves, and top with the diced feta cheese and a few oregano leaves.

• Drizzle the olive oil and a squeeze of fresh lemon juice over the top.

Make your own

Feel free to make up your own salads, too—even a simple mix of crunchy green salad leaves is delicious with a tasty homemade dressing.

leaves

tomatoes

fresh herbs

olives

3

Potato salad

If you like hot and spicy flavors, add 1 tbsp of horseradish sauce in step 2.

Ingredients

This recipe is for 6 people. It takes 10 minutes to prepare and 20 minutes to cook.

- 3lb (1¼kg) new potatoes
- ¼ cup mayonnaise
- 2 tbsp sour cream
- 2 tbsp chopped fresh chives

Method

- Cook the new potatoes in boiling water for 15–20 minutes, or until tender when pierced with a sharp knife. Drain and let cool.
- Mix the mayonnaise with the sour cream and fresh chives in a large bowl.
- When the potatoes are cool, cut them into bite-sized pieces. Stir into the mayonnaise mixture.

4

Coleslaw

This colorful recipe makes a tasty side dish. Try it on the side of sandwiches, burgers, or chicken. It's also a great baked-potato topping!

Ingredients

This recipe is for 4 people. It takes 5 minutes to prepare and 4 minutes to cook.

- 3 tbsp plain yogurt
- ½ tbsp Dijon mustard
- 3 tbsp mayonnaise
- ½ a white cabbage
- 2 large carrots
- ½ an onion, sliced
- freshly ground black pepper

Method

- To make the dressing, mix the plain yogurt with the Dijon mustard and mayonnaise.
- Finely slice the white cabbage, grate the carrots, and mix with the sliced onion.
- Place all the vegetables in a large bowl, and stir in the dressing.
- Season to taste with freshly ground black pepper.

LIGHT BITES

Bruschetta

Bruschetta is a tasty Italian appetizer

or snack. It is traditionally made by piling ripe tomatoes onto toasted garlic bread.

40 mins   5 mins   Serves 2

Ingredients

- 4 x 1in (2.5cm) slices Italian style bread, such as ciabatta
- 3 medium-sized ripe tomatoes
- 1 tbsp olive oil
- 6 basil leaves
- 1 clove garlic, peeled

Equipment

- knife
- cutting board
- metal spoon
- sieve
- bowl
- grill pan

Halve and seed the tomatoes. Press the seeds through a sieve over a bowl, then discard the seeds. Dice the tomatoes and add to the bowl.

Add the olive oil, salt, and freshly ground black pepper. Let stand for 30 minutes. Roll up the basil leaves, chop finely, then add to the mixture.

Toast the bread on both sides, preferably in a grill pan to create dark lines, or under a preheated broiler.

Rub the warm bread with the clove of garlic. Place each piece of bread on a plate and heap with the tomato mixture.

73

Tip

Try adding some torn mozzarella, which can also be lightly toasted under a broiler.

Four ways with brushetta

Try out these these tasty bruschettas.

1

2

Tiny tomatoes

This is a delicious combination of ingredients and flavors. The mozzarella melts in your mouth and the tomatoes are so juicy.

Ingredients

This recipe is for 4 people. It takes 5 minutes to prepare and 2 minutes to cook.

- ciabatta loaf, sliced
- 4¹/₂oz (125g) mini mozzarella balls
- 1 pint tiny tomatoes
- 8 fresh basil leaves, chopped

Method

- Toast the slices of ciabatta until golden brown. You may have 1 or 2 slices left over at the end.
- Carefully slice the tiny tomatoes in half.
- Place the mozzarella balls and tiny tomatoes on the toasted slices of ciabatta.
- Scatter chopped basil leaves on each slice of ciabatta.
- Serve as individual portions or on a large serving platter.

Crisscross ham

The salty ham and melted cheese make this bruschetta a yummy appetizer. It will be a real winner with your friends or family.

Ingredients

This recipe is for 4 people. It takes 5 minutes to prepare and 4 minutes to cook.

- ciabatta loaf, sliced
- 4¹/₂oz (125g) ham
- 6oz (170g) Cheddar cheese

Method

- Toast the slices of ciabatta until golden brown. You may have 1 or 2 slices left over at the end.
- Cut the ham into thin strips and the cheese into generous slices.
- Place the cheese slices onto the ciabatta and then add the ham in a crisscross pattern.
- Broil the bruschettas for 2 minutes, or until the cheese begins to bubble. Be careful not to overcook the ham.
- Serve as individual portions or on a large serving platter.

Make your own

Bruschetta is an Italian appetizer traditionally made of toasted bread with garlic, olive oil, salt, and pepper. You can also use these ingredients.

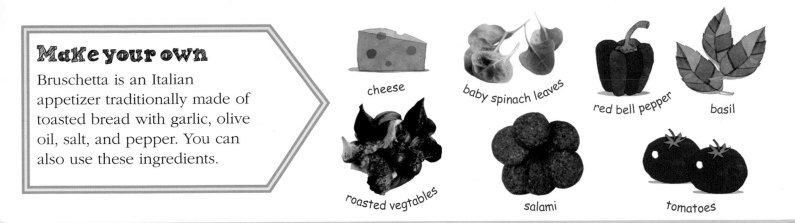

cheese

baby spinach leaves

red bell pepper

basil

roasted vegetables

salami

tomatoes

3

Carrot butter

The moist carrots and rich butter make this bruschetta a real favorite. You can keep any leftover mixture in the fridge for a few days.

Ingredients

This recipe is for 4 people. It takes 1 hour to prepare and 2 minutes to cook.

- ciabatta loaf, sliced
- 1 onion, finely chopped
- 4 carrots, finely grated
- 1 tsp tomato paste
- 1 tsp dried oregano
- 16 tbsp butter

Method

- On medium heat, fry the onions in a teaspoon of oil.

- Blend the onion, carrots, tomato paste, oregano, and butter in a food processor.

- Place the mixture in a bowl, cover, and refrigerate for 1 hour.

- Toast the slices of ciabatta until golden brown. You may have 1 or 2 slices left over.

- Generously spread the carrot butter onto the slices of toasted ciabatta and serve as individual portions or on a large platter.

- Garnish with cilantro, if desired.

4

Cheese and cucumber

These bright and fun bruschettas are great for a party. Use the remaining cucumber to make sticks to accompany the dish.

Ingredients

This recipe is for 4 people. It takes 5 minutes to prepare and 4 minutes to cook.

- ciabatta loaf, sliced
- 7oz (200g) cream cheese
- 1 cucumber

Method

- Toast the slices of ciabatta until golden brown. You may have 1 or 2 slices left over at the end.

- Spread the cream cheese evenly over the bruschettas.

- Using a knife, carefully peel a cucumber. Use cookie cutters to make decorative shapes out of the peel and flesh of the cucumber.

- Place the shapes on the bruschettas and serve on individual plates or a large serving platter.

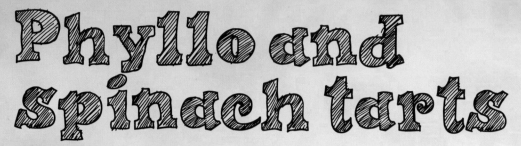

Phyllo and spinach tarts

The soft and creamy filling contrasts with the light crispy layers of phyllo pastry in this mouthwatering recipe for cheese and spinach tarts.

15 mins   25 mins   Serves 4

Ingredients

- 1 tbsp sunflower oil
- 3½oz (100g) baby spinach leaves, washed
- 4oz (125g) cream cheese
- 1oz (25g) Cheddar or Parmesan cheese, grated
- 1 medium egg, beaten
- Salt and freshly ground black pepper
- 16 x 5in (12.5cm) squares phyllo pastry

Equipment

- pastry brush
- 6-hole muffin pan
- cutting board
- sharp knife
- large mixing bowl
- wooden spoon
- dinner spoon
- oven mitts

1

Preheat the oven to 350°F (180°C). Use a pastry brush to apply oil to 4 muffin-pan holes. Place the spinach on a cutting board and chop coarsely, using a sharp knife.

2

Place the cream cheese in a bowl and beat with a wooden spoon until smooth. Then beat in the grated cheese and egg until well combined. Season well, then stir in the spinach.

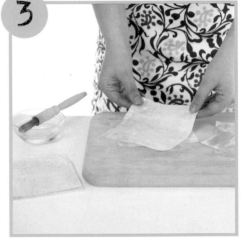

3

Brush one of the pastry squares with oil. Place another square over the top at an angle to make a star shape. Repeat with 2 more squares of pastry, brushing each with oil.

4

Gently press the layers of phyllo pastry into one of the holes of the muffin pan, then shape it to fit the hole. Repeat with the remaining pastry until you have 4 tarts.

5

Use a soup spoon to fill each crust with the spinach mixture. Press it down with the spoon. Bake for 25 minutes until the pastry has browned and the filling has set.

6

Remove the tarts from the oven and let them cool in the pan for a few minutes, then carefully remove them from the pan. Serve hot with salad or vegetables.

Rice balls

This is a fun and easy snack to make. It also works well as an appetizer for a main meal. The soft rice and melted mozzarella are yummy and have a great texture.

30 mins   5 mins   Serves 4

Ingredients

- 1¼ cups cold, cooked Arborio or other risotto rice
- ground black pepper
- 1 ball of buffalo mozzarella, cut into cubes
- 1 egg, beaten
- 2 slices toast, for bread crumbs
- olive oil, for deep frying
- salsa dip, to serve
- salad, to serve

Equipment

- mixing bowl
- large plate
- large dish
- small bowl
- sieve
- paper towels

Generously season the cold, cooked rice with black pepper. Roll the rice into 12 evenly sized balls.

Push a cube of cheese into the center of each ball, then cover so that the cheese is enclosed.

Roll each ball in the egg and then roll in the bread crumbs (toast that's been turned into crumbs in a food processor).

Ask an adult to deep-fry the balls in olive oil over medium heat for 2–3 minutes, or until golden brown.

Variation

Buy a salsa dip to serve with the rice balls. You can make this dish into a light meal by adding vegetables. Try a fresh garden salad with cherry tomatoes and cucumber slices.

Bell pepper hummus

20 mins **5 mins** **Serves 2**

Ingredients
- 2 red bell peppers
- 5½oz (150g) canned chickpeas
- 1 tsp paprika
- 1 clove garlic, peeled
- juice of ½ lemon
- 1 tbsp tahini
- 3 tbsp olive oil
- salt and pepper
- bell pepper shells, to serve

Equipment
- sharp knife
- cutting board
- baking sheet
- silver foil
- plastic bag
- food processor
- small spoon

Bell peppers and hummus make a tasty combination. So here's a recipe for red pepper hummus. The bell peppers themselves can be used as delicious little serving dishes.

1

Cut each bell pepper into 4 and remove the ribs and seeds. Preheat the broiler to high.

2

Line a baking sheet with foil and place the peppers skin side up. Broil for 5 minutes, or until the skins are blackened.

3

Put the hot peppers into a plastic bag and seal it. When the peppers are cool enough to handle, peel off the blackened skins.

4

Put the peppers, chickpeas, paprika, garlic, lemon juice, tahini, and olive oil in a food processor and blend until smooth. Season to taste.

5

Spoon the hummus into bell pepper shells and serve.

Tip

Serve the hummus with pita bread and carrot and cucumber sticks. Don't forget to eat the bell pepper containers!

Shrimp skewers

Try this filling and healthy dish. It's fun to create and tastes delicious. If you don't like shrimp, you can use chicken instead.

25 mins, plus chilling   15 mins   Serves 4

Ingredients

- ½ a red bell pepper
- ½ a yellow bell pepper
- 1 small zucchini
- ½ red onion
- 8 cherry tomatoes
- 5½ oz (150g) cooked and peeled jumbo shrimp
- salad to serve (optional)

For the marinade

- juice of 1 lemon
- juice of 1 lime
- 2 tbsp soy sauce (reduced salt)
- 1 garlic clove, crushed or finely chopped
- 1 tsp light brown sugar

Equipment

- 4 kebab skewers
- rectangular dish that will hold the length of the skewers

Make the marinade by mixing the ingredients in a bowl. Carefully cut the bell peppers and onion into chunks.

Chop the ends of the zucchini off, then carefully slice the zucchini into bite-sized chunks.

Thread the vegetables and shrimp onto the skewers. Place the kebabs in a rectangle dish.

Pour the marinade over the kebabs. Put the kebabs into the fridge for an hour. Turn them over after 30 minutes.

Ask an adult to broil the kebabs for 15 minutes. Baste the shrimp every 5 minutes with the marinade (discard any leftover marinade).

40 mins, plus marinating   15 mins   Serves 4

Ingredients

- 12 skinless, boneless chicken thighs
- 1 red and 1 yellow pepper, seeded and cut into chunks

Barbecue Sauce

- 6 tbsp ketchup
- 2 tbsp maple syrup or honey
- 2 tbsp dark soy sauce
- grated zest and juice of 1 lime
- 2 tsp freshly grated ginger
- 2 tbsp brown sugar

Equipment

- small saucepan
- wooden spoon
- cutting board
- knife
- mixing bowl
- small wooden skewers (soaked in water for 30 minutes)
- pastry brush

1

Place all the ingredients for the sauce in a small pan, bring to a boil, then simmer for 2 minutes, stirring until the sugar has dissolved. Let cool.

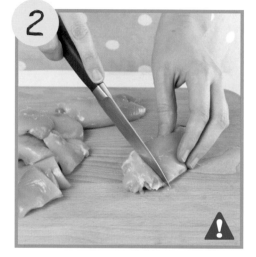

2

Cut each chicken thigh into 2 to 3 pieces. Place the cooled sauce in a large bowl. Turn the cutting board over.

3

Add the chicken, stir to coat, then let marinate for about 30 minutes.

4

Thread 2 to 3 pieces of chicken onto wooden skewers with pieces of red and yellow bell pepper. Repeat until the chicken and peppers have been used up.

5

Line the bottom of a broiler pan with foil, then broil for 10–12 minutes, turning and brushing with the sauce, until the chicken is thoroughly cooked.

BBQ chicken skewers

These bite-sized skewers are a tasty option. Make double quantities of the sauce and use half for dipping if you like.

Tip

Remember to soak the wooden skewers in water for 30 minutes to prevent them from burning.

Four ways with Kebabs

Kebabs are fun and really easy to make.

1

2

Chicken satay

This is a popular kebab recipe. Always soak the wooden skewers in cold water for 30 minutes to prevent them from burning.

Ingredients

This recipe is for 4 people. It takes 20 minutes to prepare and 16 minutes to cook.

• 1lb (450g) chicken breasts

• 1/2 lime, cut into wedges, to serve

> To make sure the chicken is fully cooked, pierce it with a fork to see if the juices run clear.

Method

• Make up the satay sauce in a large bowl and set aside. Save a small amount to use as a dip.

• Cut up the chicken breasts into large chunks 1 1/2in (4cm) cubes and place into the large bowl of satay sauce. Marinate in the fridge for 1 hour.

• Thread the chicken chunks onto short skewers (or large skewers cut in half). Discard any remaining marinade.

• Place the kebabs on a grill pan and cook for about 8 minutes. Turn over and cook for another 8 minutes. Serve the chicken warm with the satay sauce for dipping and wedges of lime.

Ingredients

This recipe is for 4 people. It takes 80 minutes to prepare and 20 minutes to cook.

For the kebabs

• 9oz (250g) firm tofu

• 2 small zucchini, each cut into 8 wedges

• 2 medium red onions, each cut into 8 wedges

• 1 medium red bell pepper, seeded and cut into 16 chunks

For the marinade

• 2 tbsp olive oil

• 1 tbsp soy sauce

• 3 tbsp black bean sauce

• 1 tbsp honey

• 2 garlic cloves, crushed

• salad, to serve

Tofu chunks

This colorful kebab would make a perfect vegetarian option for a summer barbecue.

Method

• Cut the tofu into 16 cubes. Put the cubes into a dish with the zucchini, onions, and red bell pepper.

• Mix the ingredients for the marinade in a large dish. Season. Use a spoon to coat the tofu and vegetables in the marinade. Put in the fridge for 1 hour.

• Thread the vegetables and tofu onto 8 skewers.

• Place the kebabs on the grill and brush them with the marinade. Grill for 15–20 minutes, turning them halfway through and brushing them with more marinade.

yellow zucchini
mushrooms
onions
halloumi cheese
eggplant

Try your own

Play around with combinations of ingredients to make up your own kebabs. Use the barbecue sauce to create a beef and onion one. You can use the items pictured here, although not all on one kebab!

3

4

Lamb with mint

Lamb is delicious when flavored with herbs and spices. You can make a mint and yogurt dip to accompany this classic kebab.

Ingredients

This recipe is for 4 people. It takes 20 minutes to prepare and 20 minutes to cook.

• 1lb (450g) ground lamb

• 1 small onion, finely chopped

• 1 garlic clove

• ½ tsp ground cinnamon

• 2 tsp ground cumin

• 1 tsp ground coriander

• olive oil, for brushing

• 1 tsp dried mint

• ½ lemon, to serve

Method

• Put the ground lamb in a mixing bowl. Add the chopped onion, garlic, cinnamon, cumin, and coriander to the bowl. Stir the ingredients until they are all combined.

• Divide the lamb mixture into 12 pieces. Shape each one into a sausage and then thread them onto the skewers. Press or roll to lengthen the kebabs.

• Place the lamb kebabs onto the baking sheet and brush them with oil. Grill them for about 5 minutes on each side, until golden. Transfer to a serving dish and sprinkle with mint.

Ingredients

This recipe is for 4 people. It takes 25 minutes to prepare and 15 minutes to cook.

For the marinade

• juice of 1 lemon

• juice of 1 lime

• 2 tbsp soy sauce

• 1 garlic clove, crushed

• 1 tsp light brown sugar

For the kebabs

• ½ red bell pepper

• ½ yellow bell pepper

• 8 cherry tomatoes

• 4 baby corn

• 5½ oz (150g) cooked shrimp

Shrimp and peppers

These bright and colorful kebabs are full of flavor. Squeeze lime juice on them to serve.

Method

• Make the marinade by mixing the ingredients in a pitcher. Carefully cut the bell peppers and baby corn into chunks.

• Thread the vegetables and shrimp onto the skewers. Place the kebabs into a rectangular dish. Pour the marinade over the kebabs. Put the kebabs into the fridge for an hour. Turn them over after 30 minutes.

• Grill the kebabs for 15 minutes. Baste the shrimp every five minutes with the marinade (discard any leftover marinade).

Zucchini frittata

Ciao! This recipe is not just an ordinary omelet, but an Italian one filled with your homegrown vegetables. Buon appetito! (Have a good meal!)

25 mins   40 mins   Serves 8

Ingredients

- 1lb (450g) new potatoes
- 4 tbsp butter
- 1 large onion, finely chopped
- 3 zucchini, thinly sliced
- 1 tbsp fresh mint leaves, chopped
- 8 eggs
- 3oz (75g) Pecorino cheese
- a pinch of ground black pepper

Equipment

- large saucepan
- colander
- knife
- cutting board
- large frying pan
- wooden spoon
- small bowl
- fork
- ladle

Cook the potatoes in boiling water for 15-20 minutes, or until tender. Use a colander to drain them. Let them cool, and then halve those that are large.

Melt the butter in an 11in (28cm) diameter, nonstick frying pan. Add the onion and cook gently until soft. Add the zucchini and cook. Stir often.

Stir in the potatoes and continue cooking for another 5 minutes, until the zucchini has softened.

Crack the eggs into a bowl and add the Pecorino and mint and season well with pepper. Whisk together using a fork.

Pour the egg mixture into the pan and turn the heat down as low as possible. Cook for 5 minutes, until the eggs are just set.

Place the pan under a preheated broiler for 5 minutes to brown the top. When ready, remove and let the frittata cool.

Ingredients

- 12oz (375g) store-bought puff pastry
- 9oz (250g) cherry tomatoes
- 9oz (250g) ricotta cheese
- 2 large eggs, beaten
- 2 tbsp freshly chopped basil
- 1oz (25g) Parmesan cheese, grated
- Salt and black pepper

Equipment

- rolling pin
- baking sheet
- sharp serrated knife
- cutting board
- large mixing bowl
- wooden spoon
- oven mitts

Tomato and basil tart

This tart looks so impressive no one will guess how simple it is to make! Serve it with salad and crusty bread for a delicious weekend lunch.

Preheat the oven to 400°F (200°C). Using a rolling pin, roll out the pastry on a lightly floured surface to a rectangle measuring about 10 x 15in (25 x 38cm).

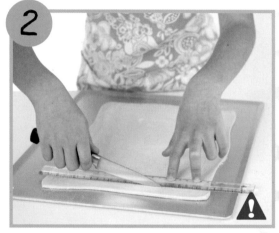

Place on a large flat baking sheet. Using a sharp knife, score a 1in (2.5cm) border along the sides of the rectangle, being careful not to cut all the way through.

Place the cherry tomatoes on a cutting board and use a sharp knife to cut the tomatoes in half. A knife with a serrated edge will make the job easier.

In a large mixing bowl, stir together the ricotta cheese, eggs, basil, and Parmesan cheese with a wooden spoon, until combined. Season with a little salt and freshly ground black pepper.

Spoon this mixture inside the marked edge and scatter over the tomatoes. Cook in the center of the oven for 20 minutes, until the pastry is risen and golden and the filling cooked.

20 mins   9 mins   Makes 24

- 2oz (50g) frozen peas, defrosted
- 5½oz (150g) fresh bread crumbs
- ¼ cup freshly chopped parsley
- 2 eggs, beaten
- sunflower oil for frying

For the lemon mayonnaise

- 1 cup reduced fat mayonnaise
- grated zest and juice of ½ lemon

Equipment

- medium saucepan or frying pan with lid
- 4 mixing bowls
- 3 metal spoons
- plate
- nonstick frying pan
- spatula

Ingredients

- 14oz (400g) fresh salmon fillets
- 14oz (400g) cooked potato

1 **Place the fish** in the pan. Add a little water and bring to a boil. Cover and cook for 5–6 minutes. Let cool, then flake, removing any skin and bones.

2 **Place the potato**, peas, and salmon in a bowl. Mix gently until combined and season to taste.

3 **Mix the bread crumbs** with the parsley and place on a plate.

4 **Place a heaping teaspoon** of the salmon mixture in your hands, roll into a ball, then flatten. Dip into the egg, then coat in the bread crumb mixture.

5 **Heat a little oil** in a frying pan and fry the fish cakes for 2–3 minutes on each side until golden.

6 **Mix together** the mayonnaise with the lemon zest and juice. Transfer to a bowl. Serve the fish cakes warm or cold on toothpicks with the dip.

Mini fish cakes

Serve these bite-sized fish cakes

on toothpicks to make them easier to dip
in the creamy lemon mayonnaise.

MAIN MEALS

Grilled chicken

Food has a wonderful texture and finish to it when it's been cooked in a grill pan. Always make sure you cook the meat thoroughly. You can eat this dish hot or cold.

Ingredients

- 2 tsp paprika
- 5 tbsp olive oil
- 4 skinless, boneless chicken breasts, each about 5½oz (150g)
- 14oz (400g) baby new potatoes, cut in half, if necessary
- 2 scallions, finely chopped
- 8 cherry tomatoes, halved
- 3 tbsp chopped fresh mint
- 1 tbsp lemon juice

Equipment

- large shallow dish
- tablespoon
- plastic wrap
- grill pan
- tongs
- small sharp knife
- cutting board
- medium saucepan
- colander
- large glass bowl

1 **Mix the paprika** and 3 tablespoons of olive oil in a large dish. Add the chicken and spoon over the marinade. Cover with plastic wrap and chill for 30 minutes.

2 **Heat a grill pan** until it is very hot. Reduce the heat to medium and place 2 chicken breasts in the pan. Grill for 6 minutes on one side.

3 **Carefully turn** the chicken over using tongs. Spoon over a little of the marinade and then cook for 6 minutes, or until cooked through. Grill the remaining chicken.

4 **Put the potatoes** in a medium saucepan and cover with water. Bring to a boil and cook the potatoes for 10 minutes, or until they are tender.

5 **Drain the potatoes** and let them cool in a bowl. Add the mint. When cool, add the tomatoes and scallions to the potatoes.

6 **Mix the olive oil** and lemon juice together, using a fork. Then pour the dressing over the salad and stir well to mix.

Four ways with roast vegetables

Each of these dishes can accompany a main meal.

1

Reds and greens

This vegetable medley is colorful and has a slight crunch. It can be paired with rice balls or grilled chicken.

Ingredients

This recipe is for 4 people when served as a side dish. It takes 8 minutes to prepare and 50–60 minutes to cook.

- 2 red onions
- 2 whole raw beets, peeled
- ½ head of broccoli
- 12 cherry tomatoes
- 1 tbsp olive oil

Method

- Preheat the oven to 400°F (200°C).
- On a cutting board, use a sharp knife to cut the red onion carefully into large chunks, slice the beets into large wedges, and cut the florets off the broccoli.
- Place the beets in a roasting pan or ovenproof dish and use your hands to toss the vegetables in oil. Cook for 20 minutes.
- Add the remaining ingredients and cook for another 30–40 minutes.

2

Sweet potato and parsnip

Perfect on a cold day, this option works nicely with hotpot recipes.

Ingredients

This recipe is for 4 people when served as a side dish. It takes 5 minutes to prepare and 50 minutes to cook.

- 4 large sweet potatoes, peeled
- 4 parsnips, peeled
- 1 tbsp olive oil

Method

- Preheat the oven to 400°F (200°C).
- On a cutting board, use a sharp knife to cut the parsnips carefully into large chunks and slice the sweet potatoes into large wedges.
- Put the parsnips and potatoes into a roasting pan or an ovenproof dish and use your hands to toss the vegetables in oil.
- Roast in the oven for 50 minutes, or until the vegetables are golden brown.

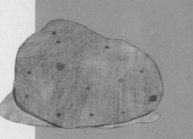

Try your own

There are plenty of other vegetables that taste delicious when roasted and work well as a side for any main dish. Try these other ingredients.

tomatoes   mushrooms   butternut squash   leeks

olives

3

Bell pepper medley

Roasted garlic is really tasty, and roasted peppers are juicy and full of flavor. This dish makes a good side for chicken dishes.

Ingredients

This recipe is for 4 people when served as a side dish. It takes 8 minutes to prepare and 40 minutes to cook.

· 1 green bell pepper

· 1 yellow bell pepper

· 1 red bell pepper

· 1 orange bell pepper

· 1 garlic clove

· 2 small zucchini

· 1 tbsp olive oil

Method

• Preheat the oven to 400°F (200°C).

• On a cutting board, use a sharp knife to slice the peppers into thin strips and cut the garlic in half.

• Carefully cut the zucchini into thick slices.

• Place all the ingredients in a roasting pan or ovenproof dish and use your hands to toss the vegetables in oil.

• Cook for 40 minutes.

4

Roast potato and carrot

This is a classic choice of roasted vegetables that often gets served with chicken. It can help add carbohydrates to a lighter meal.

Ingredients

This recipe is for 4 people when served as a side dish. It takes 5 minutes to prepare and 50 minutes to cook.

· 12 Chantenay carrots or 5 regular carrots

· 2 large potatoes, peeled

Method

• Preheat the oven to 400°F (200°C).

• On a cutting board, use a sharp knife to quarter the potatoes and cut the carrots into thick wedges.

• Scatter the potatoes and carrots in a roasting pan or ovenproof dish and use your hands to toss the vegetables in oil.

• Cook for 50 minutes, or until the vegetables are golden brown.

10 mins, plus marinating | 35-40 mins | Makes 8

Ingredients

- 1lb (500g) lamb cut into 24 x 1in (2.5cm) cubes
- 1 green bell pepper, seeded and cubed
- 1 red onion, halved

For the marinade

- ¹/₂ tsp ground cumin
- ¹/₂ tsp dried oregano
- 1 tsp olive oil
- ¹/₂ tsp ground ginger
- 3 pinches ground cinnamon
- juice of ¹/₂ orange
- 1 tbsp chopped cilantro (optional)
- 1 tbsp honey

For the couscous

- 1 tbsp olive oil
- juice of ¹/₂ orange
- ¹/₂ red onion, finely diced
- 1 cup couscous
- 1 cup stock
- ¹/₄ cup raisins
- ¹/₄ cup blanched almonds, coarsely chopped
- ¹/₂ cup dried apricots, quartered

Equipment

- 2 mixing bowls
- soup spoon
- plastic wrap
- cutting board
- sharp knife
- 8 wooden skewers
- oven mitts
- broiler and foil-lined tray
- tongs
- fork

Lamb Kebabs

This marinade adds a gentle spicy flavor to the lamb, while the couscous is very simple to cook and is a great alternative to rice.

Mix all of the marinade ingredients together in a bowl. Stir in the lamb and cover with plastic wrap. Let marinate for 1–2 hours in the fridge.

Cut each onion half into 4 equal wedges and remove the white core from each piece. Split the wedges in half to make 16 thin pieces of onion.

Place a cube of lamb onto a skewer, followed by pieces of onion and pepper. Repeat and add a piece of lamb to finish. Do the same for all 8 skewers.

Preheat the broiler. Broil the kebabs for 12–16 minutes, turning every 2–3 minutes. Let rest before serving.

5

Meanwhile, pour the hot stock over the cous cous and mix them together. Cover the bowl with plastic wrap until all the liquid has been absorbed.

6

Fluff the cooked cous cous with a fork to separate the grains. Stir in the orange juice, onion, apricots, almonds, raisins, and olive oil.

Variation

Chicken or pork are tasty alternatives to lamb. Vegetarians can add extra vegetables, such as zucchini, mushrooms, or eggplant.

20 mins 50 mins Serves 6-8

Ingredients

- 12oz (350g) store-bought pie crust
- 5oz (150g) bacon, chopped
- 3 eggs
- ¼ cup heavy whipping cream
- ¾ cup milk
- 1 tbsp freshly chopped chives
- freshly ground black pepper
- 3½oz (100g) Gruyere cheese, grated

Equipment

- rolling pin
- 9in (23cm) loose-bottomed quiche pan
- fork
- oven mitts
- parchment paper
- baking beans or aluminum foil
- nonstick frying pan
- wooden spoon
- paper towels
- large mixing bowl
- whisk
- baking sheet

Preheat the oven to 375°F (190°C). Using a rolling pin, roll out the pie crust on a lightly floured surface. Line the loose-bottomed quiche pan with the pie crust. Chill for 15 minutes.

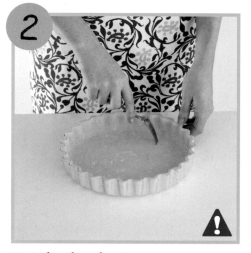

Prick the bottom with a fork, line with parchment paper and fill with baking beans or scrunched-up aluminum foil. Bake for 15 minutes. Remove the paper and beans and bake for another 5 minutes.

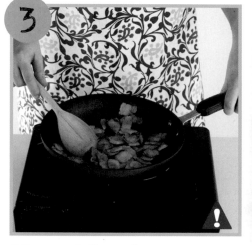

Meanwhile, place the bacon in a nonstick frying pan and cook over medium heat, stirring occasionally until it is crisp. Drain the bacon on paper towels.

In a large mixing bowl, whisk together the eggs, cream, milk, chives, and freshly ground black pepper with a whisk until they are thoroughly combined.

Place the pie crust on a baking sheet. Scatter the cooked bacon and half the cheese over the pie crust. Pour in the egg mixture, then sprinkle it with the remaining cheese.

Place the sheet in the oven and bake in the center for 25–30 minutes, until golden and set. Let cool for 5 minutes before serving in slices with salad.

Quiche Lorraine

When cooked, the cheese in this bacon-and-egg quiche melts to form a lovely crispy top. Delicious hot or cold, the quiche tastes especially good with salad.

Variation

Make a meat version by replacing the beans with 9oz (250g) lean ground beef and a small eggplant (sliced). After sweating the onion, fry the meat and eggplant until they are well-done.

Vegetarian moussaka

Traditional moussaka is made with meat and eggplant, but this vegetarian version is just as good! The pine nuts and cannellini beans give it a fantastic texture.

1

Preheat the oven to 400°F (200°C). Heat the oil in a pan over low heat. Add the onion and sweat gently until soft. Stir in the mint and one teaspoon of the oregano.

2

Add the cannellini beans, tomato sauce, and pine nuts, and bring to a boil. Reduce the heat and simmer gently until thickened.

3

Spoon the bean mixture into an ovenproof dish. In a new bowl, mix together the, egg, yogurt, and remaining oregano. Spoon the yogurt evenly over the top of the bean mixture. Bake in the oven for 15–20 minutes, until the top is golden and set.

15 mins   30 mins   Serves 4-6

Ingredients

- 1 tbsp olive oil
- 1 onion, finely chopped
- 1 tsp dried mint
- 3 tsp dried oregano
- 14oz (400g) can cannellini beans, drained and rinsed
- 24oz (700g) jar tomato sauce or 2 x 14oz (400g) cans chopped tomatoes
- ½ cup pine nuts
- 1 egg
- 1 cup Greek-style yogurt
- salad, to serve

Equipment

- frying pan
- wooden spoon
- ovenproof dish
- large spoon

Marinated chicken

The chicken in this recipe is marinated so that it absorbs the curry flavor. If you don't have time, you can skip the marinating and go straight to cooking in step 3. Alternatively, marinate longer for a more intense flavor.

20 mins, plus marinating | 10 mins | Serves 2-4

Ingredients

- 1 tsp tomato paste
- 2 tbsp vegetable oil
- 1 tbsp curry powder
- juice of $1/2$ lemon
- $1/2$ cup plain yogurt
- 2 skinless, boneless chicken breasts
- salt and pepper
- $1/4$ cup raisins (optional)
- $1/4$ cup flaked almonds (optional)
- 2 tbsp mango chutney (optional)

To Serve

- naan bread
- 1-2 little gem heads of lettuce

Equipment

- mixing bowl
- soup spoon
- 2 cutting boards
- 2 sharp knives
- frying pan
- wooden spatula

1

In a bowl, mix the tomato paste, oil, and curry powder together to make a paste. Add the lemon juice and half the yogurt to make the marinade.

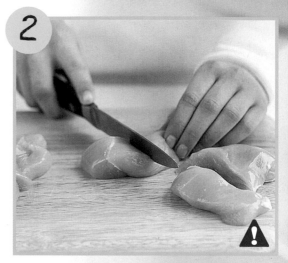

2

Carefully cut each chicken breast into cubes of about 1in (2.5cm). Turn the cutting board over.

3

Stir the chicken into the marinade, season with salt and pepper, and cover the bowl. Let the chicken marinate in the fridge for 30 minutes.

4

Place the frying pan over medium to high heat and fry the chicken for 3–4 minutes. The chicken will change color but it will not be cooked yet.

5

Add the raisins and almonds, if using, and cook for 3–4 minutes. Before serving, cut a piece of chicken in half. If there is no trace of pink, it is cooked.

6

To shred the lettuce, roll up the leaves and carefully cut them into thin slices. Serve the chicken with the shredded lettuce and naan bread.

Tip

Serve the yogurt left over from step 1 as a side dish. The plain yogurt tastes great with the curry flavor of the chicken. Stir in the mango chutney for a fruity twist.

Potato fish cakes

Potatoes can be cooked in many ways; mashed, boiled, roasted, and baked. Bite into these crunchy fish cakes and the creamy fish and potato will melt in your mouth.

⏱ 15 mins ⏲ 25 mins 🍴 Serves 4

Ingredients

- 9oz (250g) undyed smoked haddock, trimmed
- 1 fresh bay leaf
- 1¼ cups milk
- 12oz (375g) potatoes, unpeeled, boiled, and mashed
- 8 scallions, finely chopped
- 3½oz (100g) canned corn
- 4 eggs, hard-boiled, peeled and chopped
- 2 tbsp fresh parsley, chopped
- zest of 1 lemon
- ½ cup heavy cream
- 2 egg yolks

- 2 eggs
- ¾ cup flour
- 1 cup bread crumbs
- 1 tbsp butter
- 2 tbsp olive oil
- salsa, to serve
- lemon wedges, to serve

Equipment

- shallow pan
- large mixing bowl
- fork
- spoon
- 2 small glass bowls
- whisk
- cutting board
- large shallow bowl
- large plate
- frying pan
- spatula

1

Cook the haddock fillets with the bay leaf and the milk in a shallow pan. Simmer for 5–10 minutes. Cool, remove the fish's skin and any bones, and flake into chunks.

2

Mix the fish, potato, scallions, corn, chopped eggs, parsley, and zest. In a small bowl, beat the cream with the egg yolks, and stir into the mixture.

3

Divide the mixture into 4 parts. Shape each part into a slightly flattened ball. Roll each fish cake in the flour on a plate. Shaking off any excess.

4

Crack two eggs into a small bowl and whisk. Transfer to a large shallow bowl. Dip each fish cake into the eggs so that they get egg all over the surface.

5

Dip egg-coated fish cake into the bread crumbs and coat all over, then set aside. Repeat dipping into egg then bread crumbs with the remaining fish cakes.

6

Heat the oil and butter in a frying pan and add the fish cakes carefully. Cook them gently for about 4–5 minutes on each side, or until golden brown.

Tomato and eggplant layers

Slow roasted tomatoes are chewy, juicy, and tasty. Anyone who tries this dish will love the combination of textures and flavors.

40 mins   3 hrs 15 mins   Serves 4

Ingredients

- 6 large ripe tomatoes, cut in half
- 2 garlic cloves, finely chopped
- 1 tbsp dried oregano
- $\frac{1}{2}$ cup extra-virgin olive oil
- 1 large eggplant, thinly sliced
- pinch of smoked paprika
- $\frac{1}{2}$ cup plain yogurt
- 2 tbsp honey
- 4 tbsp sliced almonds, toasted

Equipment

- baking sheet
- spoon
- colander
- large bowl
- grill pan
- 4 serving dishes

1

Lay the tomatoes cut-side up on the baking sheet. In a bowl, mix the garlic and oregano, half the olive oil, and season with salt and pepper. Spoon it over the tomatoes.

2

Preheat the oven to 300°F (150°C). Bake the tomatoes for 2–3 hours. When ready, they should be slightly shrunk, but still a brilliant red color. Let cool.

3

Layer the slices of eggplant in a colander, sprinkling a little salt between each layer. Leave for 30 minutes, then rinse well with water and dry.

4

Place the eggplant slices in a large bowl, pour over the rest of the olive oil, and sprinkle with a little paprika. Toss together with your hands.

5

Heat a ridged grill pan, then add a single layer of the eggplant slices. Cook each side until tender. Place the slices on a plate. Repeat for the other slices.

6

To serve, layer the tomatoes and eggplant in 4 dishes. Drizzle 2 tablespoons of yogurt and ½ tablespoon of honey over each dish. Sprinkle 1 tablespoon of almonds over each portion.

111

Beef pasta

This pasta dish is an easy main meal to make for you and your family. The combination of beef and mushrooms tastes great.

5 mins   10 mins   Serves 4

Ingredients

- 1 small onion, finely chopped
- $1/2$ tbsp olive oil
- ground black pepper
- 9oz (250g) lean ground beef
- $3^1/_2$oz (100g) mushrooms, finely chopped
- pinch of dried oregano
- 1 garlic clove, finely chopped
- 14oz (400g) can chopped tomatoes
- 1 tbsp tomato paste
- 1 tsp green pesto
- 7oz (200g) rigatoni pasta

Equipment

- frying pan
- wooden spoon
- saucepan
- colander

Cook the onion in the oil over low heat. Season with pepper, then stir in the beef and cook, stirring, until no longer pink.

Add the mushrooms, oregano, garlic, tomatoes, and tomato paste and stir well. Simmer for 10 minutes, then stir in the pesto.

Cook the pasta in a saucepan of boiling water according to the package instructions.. Using a colander, drain the pasta (over a bowl or sink), toss with the meat sauce, and serve.

Fresh tomato pasta

You don't need to cook the sauce for this pasta dish. It's deliciously fresh and fast to make. The classic flavors of tomato and basil are perfect together.

5 mins　10 mins　Serves 4

Ingredients

- 5 tomatoes, seeded and coarsely chopped
- 2 garlic cloves, finely chopped
- handful of basil leaves, torn
- 2 tbsp extra virgin olive oil
- ground black pepper
- 7oz (200g) farfalle pasta
- Parmesan cheese, freshly grated, to serve

Equipment

- large glass bowl
- wooden spoon
- large saucepan
- colander

Put the tomatoes, garlic, basil, and olive oil in a large bowl and season with black pepper. Stir the mixture together using a wooden spoon.

Cook the pasta in a saucepan of boiling water according to the package instructions. Using a colander, drain the pasta well, then toss with the tomato sauce and serve.

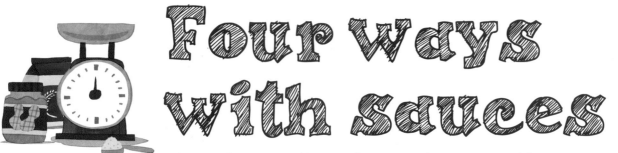

Four ways with sauces

Try these simple and versatile sauces.

1

Chunky tomato sauce

This sauce is hearty and full of flavor.
It can be used in a lasagne if you double the
quantities or as a simple sauce for a pasta dish.

Ingredients

This recipe is for
4 people. It takes
3 minutes to prepare
and 5 minutes to cook.

• 1 onion

• 1 garlic clove

• 2 tbsp olive oil

• 14oz (400g) can
 tomatoes

• 1 tbsp tomato paste

Method

• Chop the onion into small
pieces and peel and crush
the garlic clove.

• Pour the oil into a saucepan
and add the onion and garlic.
Fry gently for 2 minutes, or
until the onion is golden.

• Add the canned tomatoes
and paste to the saucepan,
stir, then cook for 3 minutes.

2

Crunchy satay sauce

You can use smooth peanut butter for this
classic sauce, but crunchy peanut butter
gives it a better texture.

Ingredients

This recipe is for
4 people. It takes
5 minutes to prepare
and 6 minutes to cook.

• 1½ onions

• 1½ in (3cm) cube
fresh ginger

• 3 garlic cloves

• ¼ cup vegetable oil

• 3 tbsp soy sauce

• ²/₃ cup water

• ¼ cup light
brown sugar

• 1 cup crunchy
peanut butter

• juice of 2 limes

Method

• Peel the onion and
chop it very finely.

• Peel the ginger and grate
it coarsely, then peel and
crush the garlic.

• Heat the oil in a saucepan.
Cook the onion gently for
3 minutes, or until soft. Add
the ginger and garlic and cook
for a few minutes. Let the
mixture cool.

• Put the onion mixture, soy
sauce, water, sugar, peanut
butter, and lime juice in a
bowl and whisk.

As the name suggests, a saucepan is used for making sauces. You will need these items to make most sauces. The wooden spoon is for stirring, and the whisk is for blending the ingredients.

saucepan

wooden spoon

whisk

knife

3

4

Cheesy white sauce

This sauce is often used in lasagne. You can also put it on pasta and add cooked bacon to make a cheesy, creamy pasta.

Ingredients

This recipe is for 6 people (when used in a lasagne). It takes 5 minutes to prepare and 6 minutes to cook.

• 4 tbsp unsalted butter

• ¼ cup all-purpose flour

• 2 cups warm milk

• 2oz (60g) Parmesan cheese, grated

Method

• Over low heat, melt the butter in a small pan.

• Stir in the flour and cook for 1 minute. Gradually whisk in the milk. Stir and continue heating until thickened.

• Add the cheese and season. Stir until the cheese is mixed into the sauce.

Barbecue sauce

Tasty and sweet, this sauce uses the natural sugars from oranges and honey to give it a delicious flavor.

Ingredients

This recipe is for 6 people. It takes 10 minutes to prepare and works perfectly for a marinade.

• 2 garlic cloves

• ¼ cup ketchup

• ¼ cup soy sauce

• ¼ cup fresh orange juice

• 2 tbsp sunflower oil

• 6 tbsp honey

• 2 tsp mustard

Method

• Crush the garlic cloves and put in a glass bowl.

• Add the ketchup, soy sauce, and orange juice to the bowl and mix well with a wooden spoon.

• Pour in the sunflower oil, honey, and mustard. Mix all the ingredients for 2 minutes, or until everything has blended into a sauce.

• Use it as a marinade to flavor meat or vegetables.

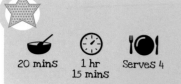

20 mins | 1 hr 15 mins | Serves 4

Ingredients

- 4 medium tomatoes, quartered
- 1 red onion, cut into 8 wedges
- 3 sweet potatoes, (about 1lb [450g]), peeled and sliced
- 2 zucchini, sliced
- 1 red bell pepper, seeded and cubed
- 1 yellow bell pepper, seeded and cubed
- 18oz (500g) ricotta cheese
- 1 tbsp olive oil
- 3 tbsp freshly chopped basil
- 3½oz (100g) Cheddar cheese, grated
- ½ cup heavy cream
- 1 egg, beaten
- 8 sheets fresh lasagne (about 4oz [125g])

Equipment

- cutting board
- knife
- 3 mixing bowls
- roasting pan
- metal spoon
- large ovenproof dish

1

Preheat the oven to 350°F (180°C). Place all the vegetables in a bowl and add the olive oil. Season with salt and freshly ground black pepper.

2

Place the vegetables in a roasting pan. Cook for 40 minutes, stirring occasionally until tender.

3

In a bowl, combine the ricotta with the cream, basil, half the cheese, and the egg.

4

Arrange half the vegetables in the bottom of an ovenproof dish, place half the lasagne sheets over the top, then spoon over half the ricotta mixture.

5

Repeat once more, finishing with a layer of the cheese mixture. Sprinkle over the remaining cheese and bake for 35–40 minutes, until golden and bubbling.

Sweet potato lasagne

This lasagne is lighter than a traditional lasagne. Ricotta cheese mixed with fresh basil replaces the traditional béchamel sauce.

Tip

Use fresh lasagne sheets, since there is no sauce for dried sheets to absorb.

Chili con carne

This dish has a kick to it, so if you don't like your food too spicy then use less of the chile and chili powder. You can serve it with tortilla chips, salsa, and guacamole.

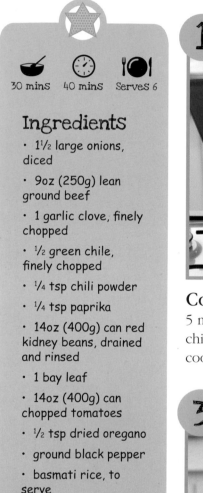

30 mins 40 mins Serves 6

Ingredients

- 1½ large onions, diced
- 9oz (250g) lean ground beef
- 1 garlic clove, finely chopped
- ½ green chile, finely chopped
- ¼ tsp chili powder
- ¼ tsp paprika
- 14oz (400g) can red kidney beans, drained and rinsed
- 1 bay leaf
- 14oz (400g) can chopped tomatoes
- ½ tsp dried oregano
- ground black pepper
- basmati rice, to serve

Equipment

- frying pan
- wooden spoon
- sharp knife
- cutting board
- colander
- small bowls

1

Cook the onions and meat for 5 minutes. Stir in the garlic, chile, chili powder, and paprika, and cook for 5 minutes.

2

Add the kidney beans and bay leaf, and fry for 2 minutes.

3

Add the tomatoes and oregano. Bring to a boil, season with pepper, then simmer on low heat for 40 minutes, stirring occasionally.

4

Cook the rice according to the package instructions. Drain using a colander. Take the bay leaf out of the chili. Serve the chili over rice.

Tip

Ask an adult
to cut up the chile.
It can sting your eyes
if you accidentally
touch them.

Fish and wedges

Fish and "chips" is a traditional British favorite. You can make sweet potato wedges instead of the fries that normally accompany this dish.

30 mins   35 mins   Serves 4

Ingredients

- 1 cup all-purpose flour
- 1 tsp baking soda
- 1 tsp paprika
- ⅔ cup cold carbonated water
- Pinch of black pepper
- 1 cup sunflower oil
- 10oz (300g) white fish, such as pollack or haddock, cut into ½ in (1cm) strips

For the sweet potato wedges

- 2 large sweet potatoes
- 2 tbsp olive oil

Equipment

- sharp knife
- large baking pan
- pastry brush
- large mixing bowl
- whisk
- deep-sided frying pan
- slotted spoon
- paper towels

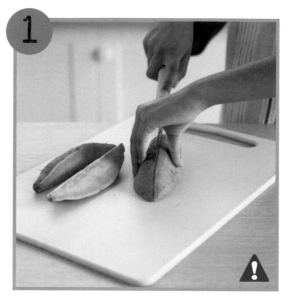

Preheat the oven to 400°F (200°C). Wash the sweet potatoes and carefully slice them into wedges.

Place the wedges in an large baking pan and brush olive oil over them. Roast them for 25 minutes, or until lightly browned.

Put the flour, baking soda, paprika, and carbonated water in a mixing bowl, season with black pepper, then whisk until smooth.

Ask an adult to heat the sunflower oil in a deep-sided frying pan. Coat the fish in the batter.

5

Ask an adult to cook the fish until it's golden brown. Remove the fish with a slotted spoon. Drain on paper towels.

Veggie quiche

⏱ 1 hr 15 mins. plus chilling 🕐 1 hr 5 mins 🍴 Serves 4-6

Ingredients

- 1½ cups all-purpose flour, plus extra for rolling
- 1 pinch of salt
- 6 tbsp unsalted butter, diced
- 2 tbsp vegetable shortening or lard, cubed
- 2 tbsp water
- 2 eggs, beaten
- ½ cup light cream
- 4oz (125g) corn
- 4oz (125g) peas
- 1oz (30g) cheese, grated
- 3½oz (100g) ham, cubed
- ½ cup milk
- 1 small leek, sautéed

Equipment

- sieve
- mixing bowl
- fork
- tablespoon
- plastic wrap
- rolling pin
- 8in (20cm) loose-bottomed, fluted pie pan
- butter knife
- parchment paper
- baking beans or dried kidney beans
- oven mitts
- liquid measuring cup
- whisk

This is a simple introduction to making savory pie dough. Here's a top tip—when making either savory or sweet pie dough, make sure that your hands are not too hot and that the butter and water are also cool so that the dough has a light texture.

Sieve the flour and salt into a bowl. Using a fork, gently stir the diced butter and vegetable shortening into the flour until they are completely coated.

Rub the butter and shortening into the flour with your fingertips, until it looks like coarse bread crumbs. Preheat the oven to 400°F (200°C).

Add the water, drop by drop, and stir it into the crumbs with a butter knife. When the crumbs start to stick together in lumps, gather the dough in your hands.

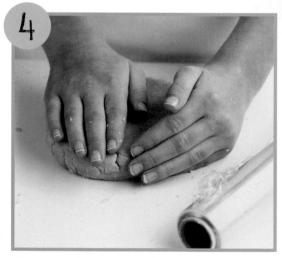

Shape the dough into a smooth disk and wrap it in plastic wrap. Chill it for 1 hour, or until firm. Lightly flour the work surface.

Roll out the dough so that it is slightly bigger than the pan. Gently press it into the pan and trim off the excess. Prick the bottom and chill it for 15 minutes.

Cover the quiche with 2 layers of parchment paper and add the baking beans. Bake for 15 minutes, remove the paper and beans, and bake for 5 minutes.

Reduce the oven to 350°F (180°C). Scatter the ham and vegetables over the bottom. Whisk the eggs, milk, and cream and pour on top. Bake for 45 minutes. Let cool.

Mixed bean stir-fry

This vegetarian stir-fry is incredibly tasty and quick to cook. The dried coconut and cashew nuts give it a crunchy texture and delicious flavor.

30 mins,
plus soaking   10 mins   Serves 4

Ingredients

- 1/3 cup dried coconut, unsweetened
- 2 tbsp sunflower oil
- 1 garlic clove, sliced
- 6 scallions, chopped
- 1 fennel bulb, sliced, core removed
- 1lb (450g) Haricot vert and green beans, thinly sliced
- 2 tbsp soy sauce
- 1 tbsp rice vinegar
- 3½oz (100g) bean sprouts
- 1tbsp cilantro, chopped
- 7oz (200g) whole wheat noodles
- 1 tbsp sesame seeds
- ½ cup unsalted cashew nuts

1

Place the coconut in a bowl of warm water, cover, and leave for 20 minutes. Strain the coconut through a sieve, pressing it against the sides.

2

Heat the oil in a large frying pan or wok. Add the garlic, onion, and fennel. Using a wooden spoon, stir all the time for about 2 minutes.

3

Add your sliced beans and fry quickly, stirring all the time. Pour on the soy sauce and vinegar. Stir in, then remove the pan from the heat.

4

Add the bean sprouts to the stir-fry. Sprinkle on the coconut and cilantro. Then stir the mixture well.

5

Cook the noodles following the instructions on the package. Drain the noodles using a colander, then spoon them into your serving bowls.

6

Spoon the stir-fry on top of the noodles. After roasting the cashew nuts and sesame seeds, sprinkle over the top and serve.

Rainbow beef

15 mins, plus marinating • 10 mins • Serves 4

Ingredients
- 10oz (300g) lean beef, cut into thin strips
- 1 tbsp sunflower oil
- 1 red bell pepper, seeded and cut into thin strips
- 6 baby corn, halved
- 2½oz (75g) snow peas
- 3 scallions, sliced on the diagonal
- 2 cloves garlic, chopped
- 2 tsp grated fresh ginger
- ¼ cup fresh orange juice

Marinade
- 6 tbsp hoisin sauce
- 2 tbsp soy sauce
- 1 tbsp honey
- 1 tsp sesame oil

Equipment
- small sharp knife
- cutting board
- spoon
- shallow dish
- wok or large frying pan
- spatula or wooden spoon
- tongs

Stir-frying is a quick and easy way to make a colorful and nutritious meal. You can serve it on its own or eat it with rice or noodles.

Put the marinade ingredients in a shallow dish. Mix them together and then add the beef strips. Coat them in the marinade, cover, and set aside for 1 hour.

Heat the sunflower oil in a wok or frying pan. Remove the beef from the marinade using tongs and carefully put it into the wok or frying pan.

Stirring continuously, fry the beef on high heat for 1½ minutes, or until browned all over. Remove the beef using the tongs and set aside.

Add a little more oil to the wok if it looks dry. Add the red bell pepper, baby corn, snow peas, and scallions. Stir-fry for 2 minutes.

5

Add the garlic, ginger, beef, and leftover marinade and stir-fry for 1 minute. Pour in the orange juice, and cook stirring, for another minute.

Variations
Strips of pork and chicken are a good alternative to the beef, or you can try shrimp or tofu. For the best flavor, it's important to marinate them first.

Marinated lime chicken

The zingy lime and fresh cilantro give this dish a delicious combination of refreshing flavors. Serve with potatoes and your choice of vegetables.

15 mins, 30 mins   Serves 4
plus marinating

Ingredients

- 4 skinless, boneless chicken breasts
- 2 eggs
- 2 cups bread crumbs
- 4 tbsp sunflower oil, for frying (1 tbsp per chicken breast)
- potatoes and beans, to serve

For the marinade

- juice of 4 limes, plus 1 lime finely sliced
- handful of cilantro, finely chopped
- 2 garlic cloves, peeled and finely sliced

Equipment

- sharp knife
- cutting board
- mixing bowls
- large frying pan
- spatula

1

Carefully make 4 small cuts on the top of each chicken breast to help marinate flavor into the meat.

2

Make the marinade by mixing all the ingredients in a bowl. Place the chicken in the marinade. Cover the bowl with plastic wrap. Chill for 1 hour in the fridge.

3

Beat the eggs in a bowl and place one piece of chicken in the bowl. Turn the chicken breast so it gets covered in egg.

4

Coat the chicken breast in bread crumbs. Repeat steps 3 and 4 for each piece of chicken. Discard any remaining marinade.

5

Fry the chicken in oil on a medium heat for 10-15 minutes on each side. Chicken needs to be cooked through, with no sign of pink.

15 mins 40 mins Serves 4

Chicken and ham pies

These yummy pies contain tender chicken and ham, cooked in a creamy sauce and topped with golden pie dough.

Ingredients

- 2 tbsp butter
- 2 tbsp all-purpose flour
- 1 cup chicken stock
- ½ cup milk
- 2 tbsp crème fraîche
- 1 tsp dried mixed herbs
- salt and black pepper
- 1 tbsp vegetable oil
- 1 small onion, sliced
- 12oz (350g) chicken breast, cubed
- 4oz (125g) cooked ham, cubed
- 3½oz (100g) frozen peas
- 12oz (350g) store-bought pie dough
- 1 egg, beaten

Equipment

- medium saucepan with lid
- whisk
- frying pan
- wooden spoon
- 4 individual pie dishes
- rolling pin
- sharp knife
- pastry brush
- oven mitts

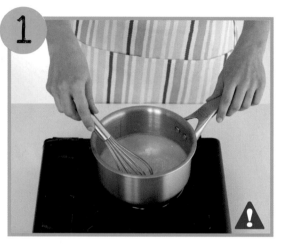

Place the butter, flour, stock, and milk in a medium saucepan. Cook over moderate heat, and continue whisking with the whisk until the mixture starts to thicken.

Bring to a boil, then reduce the heat and add the crème fraîche and herbs. Season to taste with salt and freshly ground black pepper, then simmer for 2–3 minutes.

Heat the oil in a frying pan and add the chicken and onion. Cook for 3–4 minutes, stirring occasionally, until the onion has softened and the chicken has browned.

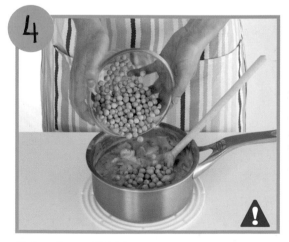

Stir the chicken and onions into the sauce, then cover and simmer for 10 minutes. Remove the pan from the heat and stir in the ham and peas.

Preheat the oven to 400°F (200°C). Let the mixture cool slightly, then divide it between four small individual pie dishes or one large one.

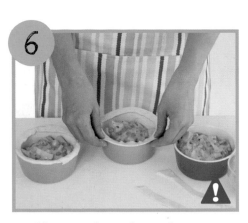

Roll out the dough on a lightly floured surface, then cut out four circles, slightly larger than the top of the pie dishes. Use the scraps to make thin strips to cover the edges of the pie dishes.

Brush the edges of the pie dishes with the egg, then press on the strips of pie dough. Brush with egg again, then place the pie lids on top. Use your fingers to seal the edges of dough together.

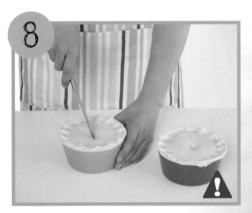

Brush the tops with egg and make a cross in the top of each pie to allow the steam to escape. Cook for 20 minutes at the top of the oven, until the pie crust is puffed and golden.

Variation

Use vegetable stock in step 1. In steps 3 and 4, omit the chicken and ham. Simmer the sauce for 5 minutes and add 12oz (350g) cooked potatoes, carrots, and parsnip, and 3oz (75g) corn when you add the peas.

Vegetable lasagne

Ingredients

- 2 large red onions
- 2 large carrots
- 2 large zucchini
- 2 red bell peppers, seeded
- 1 medium eggplant
- 2 yellow bell peppers, seeded
- ¼ cup olive oil
- 2 tsp chopped fresh rosemary
- 2 garlic cloves, crushed
- 14oz (400g) can chopped tomatoes
- 1 tbsp tomato paste
- 9 dried lasagne sheets

For the sauce

- 4 tbsp unsalted butter
- ¼ cup all-purpose flour
- 2 cups warm milk
- 4½oz (125g) Parmesan cheese, grated

Equipment

- cutting board
- sharp knife
- roasting pan
- oven mitts
- large saucepan
- wooden spoon
- small saucepan
- whisk
- lasagne dish 10 x 7in and 2in deep (25 x 18cm and 5cm deep)
- serving spoon

A crowd-pleasing dish that's a meal in its own right, this lasagne makes a welcome change from the meat-based one. Why not experiment with other flavors?

Preheat the oven to 425°F (220°C). Cut the onions into wedges and then chop all the other vegetables into chunks.

In the roasting pan, mix the oil, rosemary, and garlic with the vegetables and season. Roast for 35 minutes, shaking the pan occasionally.

Gently warm through the tomatoes and tomato paste in a large saucepan. Take the pan off the heat and carefully stir in the roasted vegetables.

On low heat, melt the butter in a pan. Stir in the flour. Cook for 1 min. Whisk in the milk. Stir until thickened. Add half the cheese and season.

Turn the oven down to 375°F (190°C). Spoon a third of the vegetables into the the dish and top with 3 lasagne sheets.

Add another third of the vegetables, top with another layer of lasagne, pour over half the sauce, and then the remaining vegetables.

Finally, lay on the remaining lasagne sheets and drizzle the sauce over the top. Sprinkle the cheese on top and bake for 35 minutes, or until golden and bubbling.

Jambalaya

This lightly spiced Cajun rice dish originated in Louisiana. The recipe can be easily adapted by adding your favorite vegetables or tofu.

1

Heat the oil in a large pan. Add the chorizo and onion and cook for 2–3 minutes, until the paprika oil from the chorizo is released.

2

Add the chicken and cook for 3–4 minutes, until lightly browned on all sides. Stir in the rice until coated in the oil.

3

Add the tomatoes, stock, and herbs. Cover and simmer for 15 minutes, stirring occasionally.

4

Add the bell peppers, peas, and scallions and cook, covered for another 10 minutes, until the rice is tender and most of the liquid has been absorbed.

5 mins   32 mins   Serves 4

Ingredients

- 1 tsp sunflower oil
- 3½oz (100g) dry Spanish chorizo, skin removed and chopped
- 1 onion, chopped
- 3 skinless, boneless chicken breasts, cubed
- 8oz (225g) easy-cook long-grain rice
- 14oz (400g) can chopped tomatoes
- 1½ cups hot chicken stock
- 1 tsp dried mixed herbs
- 1 red and green bell pepper, seeded and cubed
- 2oz (50g) frozen peas
- 6 scallions, chopped

Equipment

- large saucepan
- wooden spoon
- heatproof pitcher

15 mins 14 mins Serves 4

Ingredients

- 1 clove garlic, crushed
- 1in (2.5cm) piece fresh ginger, peeled and grated
- 1 tbsp light soy sauce
- 1 tbsp rice wine vinegar or sherry
- 12oz (350g) beef steak, (e.g., rump) thinly sliced
- 8oz (225g) dried egg noodles
- 1 tbsp sunflower oil
- 3oz (75g) snow peas, halved
- 3½oz (100g) small broccoli florets
- 3 scallions, sliced
- 1 red bell pepper, seeded and thinly sliced
- 3½oz (100g) bean sprouts
- 2 tbsp oyster sauce
- 2 tsp toasted sesame oil

Equipment

- mixing bowl
- metal spoon
- saucepan
- wooden spoon
- wok or frying pan

In a bowl, mix together the garlic, ginger, soy sauce, and rice wine vinegar or sherry. Add the sliced beef and stir, then let marinate for 10 minutes.

Meanwhile, cook the egg noodles. Place in a pan of boiling water and cook for 4 minutes. Turn off the heat. Drain the noodles and return to the pan to keep warm.

Heat the sunflower oil in a large wok or frying pan. Add the beef and stir-fry for 4–5 minutes, until browned.

Add the snow peas, broccoli, scallions, and pepper. Stir-fry for 2–3 minutes.

Add the noodles, bean sprouts, oyster sauce, and sesame oil, then stir-fry for another 2 minutes.

Beef chow mein

"Chow mein" means stir-fried noodles in Mandarin Chinese. You can add whatever you like. Fish, meat, tofu, shrimp, and vegetables are all delicious.

Tip
To make the dining experience authentic, use chopsticks to eat this Asian meal.

Lamb hotpot

This hotpot is a hearty main meal that is filling and tasty. The lamb and tomatoes make it juicy and the chickpeas add texture. Serve it with crusty bread rolls.

1

Put the lamb, flour, and paprika into a mixing bowl and combine well so that the lamb is coated.

2

Heat the oil in a large pan over medium heat, add the onions, and cook, stirring often, for 5 minutes. Add the lamb and cook until browned.

3

Stir in the garlic and chickpeas, and cook for 1 minute. Add the tomatoes, bring to a boil, then simmer for 15 minutes.

4

Season well with ground black pepper, stir in the spinach, and cook for 3 minutes.

25 mins   20 mins   Serves 6-8

Ingredients

- 6oz (175g) lean lamb (leg or filet), cut into ¾in (2cm) dice
- ½ tbsp all-purpose flour
- ¼ tsp paprika
- 1½ tbsp olive oil
- ½ large red onion, diced
- 1½ garlic cloves, chopped
- ½ x 14oz (400g) can chickpeas, drained and rinsed
- 14oz (400g) can chopped tomatoes
- ground black pepper
- 4½oz (125g) baby leaf spinach
- crusty bread rolls, to serve (optional)

Equipment

- mixing bowl
- large saucepan
- wooden spoon

20 mins 45 mins Serves 4

Ingredients

- 2 apples
- 2 tbsp olive oil
- 6–8 sausages, turkey, pork, beef, or vegetarian
- 1 onion, chopped
- 1 carrot, diced
- 2 cloves garlic, finely chopped
- 4oz (10g) bacon, cut into bite-sized pieces, optional
- 1 tsp mixed herbs
- 14oz (400g) canned borlotti or pinto beans, drained and rinsed
- ¼ cup canned chopped tomatoes
- 1 tbsp tomato paste
- salt and pepper
- 1¾ cups chicken or vegetable stock

Equipment

- vegetable peeler
- small sharp knife
- cutting board
- large ovenproof pan with lid or large saucepan and large casserole dish with lid
- oven mitts
- wooden spoon
- pitcher
- tongs

Carefully remove the peel of the apples using a vegetable peeler. Quarter them and remove the core. Cut the apples into bite-sized pieces and set aside.

Preheat the oven to 400°F (200°C). Heat the oil in a large saucepan or ovenproof pan and cook the sausages for 5 minutes, or until browned all over.

Remove the sausages from the pan and set aside. Put the onion and carrot into the pan and fry over medium heat for 5 minutes, stirring frequently.

Next, add the garlic, bacon, and herbs, stir well, and cook for 6 minutes. (Transfer to a large casserole dish if you aren't using an ovenproof pan.)

Add the beans, tomatoes, tomato paste, apples, and sausages and stir. Pour in the stock and bring to a boil.

Cover with a lid and place in the preheated oven. Cook for 25 minutes. The sauce will reduce and thicken and the apples will become tender.

Sausage hotpot

Fruit gives this savory dish a natural sweetness and an extra vitamin boost. You can serve this winter warmer with fluffy mashed potatoes and steamed green vegetables.

7 **Be careful** when removing the casserole dish from the oven, since the hotpot will be very hot. Season with salt and pepper. ⚠

DESSERTS

Frozen yogurt

You can use your favorite flavors to make this alternative to ice cream. What a great way to cool down on a hot summer day!

20 mins   4 hrs (freezing)   Serves 4-6

Ingredients

- ¹/₂ cup heavy cream
- ¹/₄ cup confectioners' sugar
- 2 cups plain yogurt
- 3oz (90g) chocolate chip cookies
- 3oz (90g) soft fudge
- 2oz (60g) mini marshmallows
- 2oz (60g) honeycomb (optional)

Equipment

- cutting board
- sharp knife
- mixing bowl
- sieve
- whisk
- spatula or metal spoon
- 2 plastic containers with lids

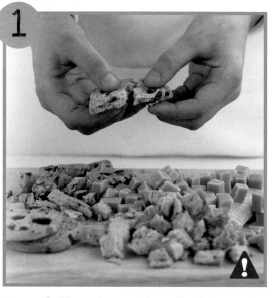

Carefully chop the fudge and honeycomb, if usuing, into tiny pieces and break the cookies into slightly larger pieces. Set aside.

Pour the cream into the mixing bowl and sift in the confectioners' sugar. Lightly whip the cream into soft peaks. (You can use an electric mixer or whisk.)

Gently fold the yogurt cookies, fudge, marshmallows, and honeycomb into the cream using a plastic spatula or metal spoon.

Spoon the mixture into the containers, cover, and freeze. Stir after 2 hours to prevent ice crystals from forming. Freeze for at least 2 hours more.

Try this recipe with 10oz (300g) of your favorite ingredients: bananas, strawberries, meringue, chocolate chips, or chopped-up candy bars.

Fruit pops

Make your own delicious frozen popsicles with this simple mix-and-match recipe. Create colorful combinations with layers of fruit, yogurt, and pure juice. These popsicles are an excellent source of vitamins and they are a great way to cool down on a hot summer day!

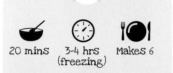

20 mins   3-4 hrs (freezing)   Makes 6

Ingredients

• 1 cup orange juice
• 10oz (300g) strawberries
• 3 large kiwis
• 3 tbsp confectioners' sugar

Equipment

• sharp knife
• cutting board
• food processor
• sieve
• wooden spoon
• 2 mixing bowls
• 6 popsicle molds
• 6 popsicle sticks
• teaspoon

1

First, rinse and drain the strawberries in cold water. Then hull and quarter the strawberries and put them into a food processor.

2

Cut a thin slice off the top and bottom of each kiwi. Working from top to bottom, carefully slice the peel off and then coarsely chop the kiwis.

3

In a food processor, blend the strawberries with 1 tablespoon of the confectioners' sugar. Sieve the purée into a bowl and throw away the seeds.

4

Wash the food processor and sieve—be careful of the blades. Blend the kiwi with 2 tablespoons of confectioners' sugar. Sieve the kiwi purée into a bowl and throw away the seeds.

5

Add the first layer and freeze for 1 hour to set. Add the next layer and push the stick gently into the first layer. Freeze for 1 hour and add the last layer.

6

Do not fill the molds all the way to the top because the mixture will expand a little as it freezes. Freeze the popsicles for a final 1–2 hours before eating.

Variation

Any fruits or fruit juices will taste great in this recipe. Add extra richness by blending 3½oz (100g) of strawberries into 10oz (300g) of flavored yogurt to make 4 creamy popsicles.

Berry alternative

If blueberries aren't your favorite, then you can use blackberries or raspberries instead. Whichever you choose, the finished result will still be a knockout.

Blueberry cheesecake

These layered desserts look impressive but are super easy to make. Presenting them in clear glasses shows off the colorful layers.

1

Place three-quarters of the berries and half of the sugar into a small saucepan. Cover and simmer for 5 minutes, or until soft. Stir in the other berries and let cool.

2

Using a clean wooden spoon, beat the cream cheese, crème fraîche, remaining sugar, and vanilla extract together in a mixing bowl. Continue until well mixed and soft.

3

Create a layered look by filling 4 glasses with a spoonful of the blueberry sauce, then a spoonful of the cream cheese mixture, and then a spoonful of the crushed cookies.

4

Repeat the layers once more and then put the filled glasses in the refrigerator for an hour to give the mixture time to set. Serve chilled straight from the fridge.

20 mins, 10 mins   Serves 4
plus setting time

Ingredients
- 18oz (500g) blueberries
- 2 tbsp sugar
- 9oz (250g) cream cheese
- ¾ cup crème fraîche
- ¼ tbsp pure vanilla extract
- 8 oat cookies, crushed

Equipment
- small saucepan
- wooden spoon
- bowl
- dessert spoon
- 4 glasses

Apple crumble

In this twist on a classic dessert, apples are cooked in a rich butterscotch sauce, topped with a crunchy, buttery crumble. Serve with custard or ice cream for the ultimate dessert!

20 mins　40 mins　Serves 4-6

Ingredients
- 1½lb (650g) apples
- ⅓ cup light brown sugar
- 2 tbsp butter
- Finely grated zest and juice of ½ lemon
- ¼ tsp salt
- ½ cup water

For the crumble
- 1 cup all-purpose flour
- 6 tbsp butter, diced
- 2 tbsp oats
- ¼ cup sugar

Equipment
- peeler
- cutting board
- corer
- sharp knife
- 1 quart ovenproof dish
- medium saucepan
- wooden spoon
- large mixing bowl
- oven mitts

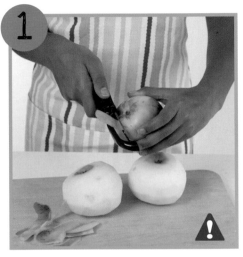

Preheat the oven to 350°F (180°C). Using a peeler, peel the apples. Place them on a cutting board and use a corer to remove the apple cores.

On the cutting board, use a sharp knife to cut the apples carefully into 1in (2.5cm) cubes. Place the pieces in the bottom of an ovenproof dish.

Place the sugar, butter, lemon zest, juice, and salt in a saucepan with the water. Bring to a boil, stirring occasionally, until the sugar has dissolved and the butter has melted.

Pour the butterscotch mixture over the chopped apples in the ovenproof dish and stir with a wooden spoon until the apples are coated evenly in the sauce.

Place the flour in a mixing bowl with the diced butter. Using your fingertips, rub in the butter until the mixture looks like rough crumbs. Stir in the oats and the sugar.

Spoon the crumble mixture over the top of the apples and bake in the oven on the top shelf for 35–40 minutes, until bubbling and golden. Let stand for 5 minutes before serving.

Fruit crumble

Crumble is a traditional English dessert and it tastes great served with cream, ice cream, or custard. Like all fruits, blackberries and peaches are a good source of vitamins, while the oats used in the crumble topping provide carbohydrates and fiber.

30 mins   35 mins   Serves 4-6

Ingredients

- 4 large ripe peaches (or 6 small ones)
- 8oz (250g) ripe blackberries
- 1/3 cup brown sugar
- 3 pinches of ground cinnamon

For the crumble

- 3/4 cup all-purpose flour
- 3/4 cup jumbo rolled oats
- 3/4 cup brown sugar
- 10 tbsp unsalted butter, diced

Equipment

- cutting board
- sharp knife
- teaspoon
- 2 mixing bowls
- metal mixing spoon
- sieve
- wooden spoon
- ovenproof dish 9 x 6in and 2in deep (23 x 15cm and 5cm deep)
- baking sheet
- oven mitts

1

Preheat the oven to 375°F (190°C). Cut round the peaches and then twist them so that they split in half. Scoop the pits out with a teaspoon.

2

Slice the halved peaches in half again and then chop each piece into 3 more chunks. Rinse and thoroughly drain the blackberries.

3

Mix the sugar and cinnamon together in a bowl. Fold in the peaches and blackberries until they are completely coated in the sugar mixture.

4

Sift the flour into a separate bowl and stir in the brown sugar. Add the oats to the bowl and stir them into the flour and sugar.

Using your fingertips, rub the diced butter into the flour mixture. The mixture should come together in small lumps when it is ready.

Place the dish on a baking sheet and spoon in the fruit filling. Scatter the topping over the fruit. Bake the crumble for 30 minutes until golden.

Variation

Other fruits such as raspberries, apples, plums, and blueberries also taste great in this recipe.

Apple pie

15 mins, plus chilling · 30-35 mins · Serves 4-6

Ingredients

- 2 cups all-purpose flour
- 1 pinch of salt
- 8 tbsp unsalted butter, diced
- 1 egg yolk, beaten with 1 tbsp water
- 2 tbsp sugar
- 1 egg, beaten, for glazing

For the filling

- 1½lb (750g) apples, peeled, cored, and cut into wedges
- 1 tsp pure vanilla extract
- ½ tsp ground cinnamon
- ⅓ cup light brown sugar
- ½ orange (zest and juice)
- 2oz (60g) chopped walnuts (optional)

Equipment

- sieve
- 2 large mixing bowls
- fork
- butter knife
- plastic wrap
- wooden spoon
- 9in (22cm) pie dish
- rolling pin
- pastry brush
- oven mitts

When making a sweet or savory pie, make a hole in the top of the pie crust before you bake it. This allows steam to escape and keeps the crust from getting soggy! Making sweet dough is very similar to making savory dough, so read the recipe carefully to note the differences!

Sift the flour and salt into a bowl and stir in the sugar. Using a fork, gently stir the diced butter into the flour until it is completely coated.

Using your fingertips, rub the diced butter into the flour. When the butter is fully mixed in, the mixture will look like coarse bread crumbs.

Stir the water and egg yolk (drop by drop) into the crumbs with a butter knife until they stick together in lumps. Gather the dough in your hands.

Put the dough onto a lightly floured work surface and shape it into a smooth disk. Wrap the disk in plastic wrap and chill it for 1 hour, or until firm.

5

Preheat the oven to 425°F (220°C). Mix the sugar, cinnamon, vanilla extract, orange juice, zest, walnuts, and apples together in a bowl.

6

Pour the filling into the dish. Dampen the edge of the dish. Roll the dough out to about ⅛in (3mm) thick and place it over the dish. Trim the excess.

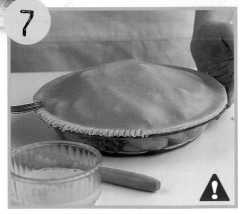

7

Press the edges of the dough into the dish and crimp with a fork. Glaze the pie with egg and make a hole in the center. Bake for 30–35 minutes, until golden brown.

Cherry and berry pie

This pie is so easy to make—you simply scrunch up store-bought pie dough and fill it with your favorite berries! You can serve it with a scoop of vanilla ice cream or whipped cream.

Ingredients

- 18oz (500g) store-bought pie dough
- 1 egg, beaten
- 2 tbsp semolina
- 1½lb (650g) mixed berries (e.g., pitted cherries, blueberries, raspberries, and blackberries)
- 2 tbsp sugar

- confectioners' sugar, for dusting

Equipment

- rolling pin
- 12in (30cm) plate
- sharp knife
- baking sheet
- pastry brush
- teaspoon
- large mixing bowl
- large metal spoon
- oven mitts

15 mins, plus chilling   30 mins   Serves 6-8

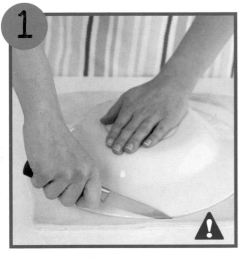

1

Preheat the oven to 400°F (200°C). Roll out the pie dough on a lightly floured surface. Cut around a 12in (30cm) plate with a sharp knife to make a circle.

2

Place the dough on a baking sheet. Use a pastry brush to spread the beaten egg on the dough, then sprinkle over 1 tablespoon of semolina with a teaspoon.

3

In a large mixing bowl, place the mixed berries, remaining semolina, and 1 tablespoon sugar. Use a large metal spoon to mix together gently, making sure not to crush the berries.

4

Pile the fruit in the center of the crust, away from the edge. Scrunch up the edges of the dough, bringing them toward the center, but leaving the middle exposed.

5

Brush the scrunched-up pie-dough edges with more beaten egg and sprinkle the dough with the remaining sugar. Chill for 30 minutes in the fridge.

6

Bake the pie on the top rack for 30 minutes, until golden. If the dough starts to become too brown, cover the pie with foil. Dust with confectioners' sugar; serve in slices.

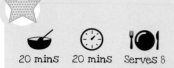

20 mins   20 mins   Serves 8

Ingredients

- 9oz (250g) graham crackers
- 8 tbsp butter

For the filling

- 8 tbsp butter, diced
- ½ cup light brown sugar
- 14oz (400g) can sweetened condensed milk
- ½ cup heavy cream
- 2 bananas, sliced

To decorate

- grated milk chocolate or flaky chocolate bar and slices of banana

Equipment

- food processor or food bag and rolling pin
- nonstick saucepan
- wooden spoon
- 8in (20cm) fluted, loose-bottomed pie pan
- large mixing bowl
- electric mixer or handheld whisk
- spoon

1

Put the graham crackers in a food processor and pulse until smooth. If you don't have a food processor, place them in a food bag and crush with a rolling pin.

2

Melt the butter for the crust in a saucepan, then stir in the crushed graham crackers with a wooden spoon. Press the mixture into the bottom and sides of the pan. Chill for 30 minutes.

3

Place the diced butter and sugar in the saucepan over low heat, and stir until the butter has melted. Add the condensed milk and gently bring to a boil, stirring continuously.

4

Boil the butter, sugar, and condensed milk for 5 minutes, stirring continuously until it is a pale caramel color. Pour over the crust and chill for 1 hour.

5

In a large mixing bowl, whip the cream with an electric mixer or whisk until it forms soft peaks. Arrange the banana slices over the toffee, then spoon over the whipped cream.

6

Decorate the top of the pie with extra sliced banana and grated milk chocolate. Serve the pie in slices. Keep chilled and eat within 2 days.

Banoffee pie

This divinely decadent caramel and banana
pie is definitely for those with a sweet tooth!

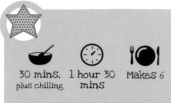

30 mins, plus chilling   1 hour 30 mins   Makes 6

Ingredients

- 18oz (500g) pumpkin, cut into chunks
- 1 tbsp olive oil
- 15oz (375g) pie dough, cut into 16 pieces
- 1 tbsp all-purpose flour
- ⅓ cup molasses
- 1 whole egg
- 3 large egg yolks
- 1¼ cups milk
- ½ split vanilla bean
- a pinch of salt
- confectioners' sugar, for dusting

Equipment

- baking sheet
- rolling pin
- bun pan
- parchment paper
- baking beans
- saucepan
- knife
- whisk
- mixing bowl
- sieve
- spoon

1

Preheat the oven to 375°F (190°C). On a baking sheet, evenly coat the pumpkin pieces with olive oil. Roast for 30 minutes, until tender. Cool and then mash with a fork.

2

Shape the dough pieces into balls. Roll out each ball until about 2½in (6cm) diameter. Press each piece into a bun pan, then chill in the fridge for 30 minutes.

3

Place a piece of parchment paper into each pie crust and fill to the top with baking beans. Bake in the oven for 15 minutes, then remove the paper and beans.

4

Pour the milk into a pan. Scrape out the vanilla seeds from the bean and add to the milk. Heat the mixture until just below boiling point. Let cool a little.

5

Lightly beat the egg yolks, whole egg, and molasses in a bowl. Add the flour and salt and beat until smooth. Strain the hot milk over the mixture and beat.

6

Pour the smooth mixture into a pan and bring to a boil, stirring all the time until thickened. Remove from heat and stir in the mashed pumpkin.

Mini pumpkin pies

Ask an adult to cut the pumpkin in half with a sharp knife, using a rocking motion. Scoop out the seeds. Slice the pumpkin into pieces, then peel it.

7

Spoon the mixture evenly into the pie crusts. Bake in the oven for 20–25 minutes, until just firm and slightly puffed up. Serve the pies warm with a dusting of confectioners' sugar on the top.

Strawberry tartlets

These pretty tartlets taste as good as they look! Make them when the fruit is in season for the best flavor, although frozen fruit will also work.

20 mins | **15 mins** | **Makes 8**

Ingredients

- 8oz (225g) store-bought pie dough
- 5oz (150g) mascarpone cheese
- ½ tsp pure vanilla extract
- 2 tbsp confectioners' sugar
- 6oz (175g) strawberries or other soft fruit
- 4 tbsp red currant jelly
- 1 tbsp water

Equipment

- rolling pin
- 3½in (9cm) fluted cookie cutter
- 12-hole bun pan
- 8 pieces of aluminum foil
- oven mitts
- cooling rack
- small mixing bowl
- wooden spoon
- sieve
- cutting board
- sharp knife
- teaspoon
- small saucepan
- pastry brush

1

Preheat the oven to 400°F (200°C). Thinly roll out the pie dough, then using a 3½in (9cm) fluted cutter, cut out 8 circles. Press the dough circles into a bun pan.

2

Press a piece of scrunched-up foil into each case. Cook for 10 minutes, then remove the foil carefully. Return to the oven for 3–4 minutes. Cool in the pan, then transfer to a cooling rack.

3

To make the filling, place the mascarpone cheese and vanilla extract in a small mixing bowl. Sift over the confectioners' sugar, then beat with a wooden spoon until smooth.

4

Place the strawberries on a cutting board. Remove the green stalks from the strawberries. Use a sharp knife to cut them in half. Quarter them if the strawberries are large.

When the pie crusts

are completely cool, use a teaspoon to fill them with the mascarpone and vanilla mixture. Arrange the strawberries on the top.

Place the red currant jelly

in a small pan with the water and cook over low heat, stirring with a wooden spoon until the jelly has dissolved. Brush this over the strawberries.

Tip

Placing scrunched-up foil in the pie crusts prevents them from shrinking.

Chocolate tart

This is perfect for chocoholics! This chocolate tart has a tangy orange pie dough base. It can be served warm or cold with a dollop of ice cream or cream.

20 mins 45 mins Serves 8

Ingredients

- 12oz (350g) store-bought pie dough
- 4 tbsp orange marmalade
- 7oz (200g) milk chocolate, broken into pieces
- 2 large eggs, beaten
- ¼ cup sugar
- ½ cup heavy cream
- cocoa powder, for dusting

Equipment

- rolling pin
- 9in (23cm) loose-bottomed pie pan
- fork
- parchment paper
- baking beans or aluminum foil
- baking sheet
- metal spoon
- heatproof bowl
- small saucepan
- large mixing bowl
- electric mixer or whisk
- wooden spoon
- oven mitts

Preheat the oven to 375°F (190°C). Using a rolling pin, roll out the dough on a lightly floured surface and use it to line the pie pan. Chill for 15 minutes.

Prick the dough with a fork, line with parchment paper and fill with baking beans or scrunched-up foil. Place on the baking sheet and bake on the top rack of the oven for 15 minutes.

Remove the paper and beans from the crust and return it to the oven for another 5 minutes, until golden. While the crust is still warm, spread the bottom with the marmalade.

Reduce the oven temperature to 325°F (160°C). Melt the chocolate in a heatproof bowl over a saucepan of simmering water, stirring constantly. Let cool slightly.

5

In a large mixing bowl, place the eggs and sugar and whisk with an electric mixer or whisk until pale and fluffy. Whisk in the chocolate until thoroughly combined.

6

Stir in the cream with a wooden spoon. Pour the mixture into the pie crust. Bake for about 25–30 minutes on the top rack of the oven until the tart has just started to set.

7

Remove the tart from the oven. It will continue to set as it cools. Dust with cocoa powder. Serve in slices with a scoop of vanilla ice cream, whipped cream, or crème frâiche.

Chocolate profitéroles

You won't be able to resist these light and fluffy profitéroles. Topped with warm chocolate sauce, they're simply delicious!

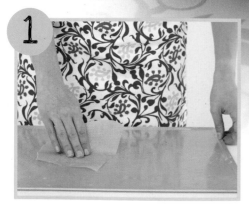

Preheat the oven to 400°F (200°C). Grease a baking sheet and sprinkle it with cold water. This will generate steam in the oven and help the dough to rise.

Place the butter and cold water in a medium saucepan and heat gently until the butter has melted. Then turn up the heat and bring them quickly to a boil.

Remove the saucepan from the heat and add all the flour at once. Then beat the melted butter and flour together with a wooden spoon until the mixture comes together.

25 mins | 25 mins | Serves 6

Ingredients

- ½ cup cold water
- 4 tbsp butter, diced
- ½ cup all-purpose flour, sifted
- 2 eggs, beaten

For the filling

- ½ tsp pure vanilla extract
- 1 cup heavy cream

For the chocolate sauce

- 4oz (125g) dark chocolate, broken into small pieces
- 2 tbsp butter
- 2 tbsp maple syrup or honey

Equipment

- baking sheet
- 2 medium saucepans
- wooden spoon
- soup spoon
- oven mitts
- knife
- electric mixer or whisk
- large mixing bowl
- teaspoon
- heatproof bowl

4 **Allow the mixture** to cool for a few minutes. Then beat in the eggs with an electric mixer or wooden spoon, a little at a time, until the mixture becomes smooth and shiny.

5 **Use a soup spoon** to place 12 golf-ball-sized dollops of the dough on the baking sheet. Bake the profiterôles on the top rack of the oven for 20–25 minutes.

6 **Using oven mitts**, take the cooked profiterôles out of the oven. Make a slit in the side of each with a knife to let the steam out, being careful not to burn your fingers. Let cool.

7 **Add the vanilla extract** and the cream to a large bowl. Whip them to form soft peaks using the electric mixer or whisk. Use the teaspoon to spoon the cream into the buns.

8 **Place the chocolate**, butter, and maple syrup or honey into a heatproof bowl. Place the bowl over a saucepan of simmering water and gently melt the contents. Stir well.

9 **Carefully spoon** the chocolate sauce over the profiterôles using a soup spoon. Serve the profiterôles immediately with any remaining sauce.

Mint chocolate pots

These luxury, rather grown-up, desserts are super-chocolatey, but with a minty kick. Dress them up with a stenciled shape of confectioners' sugar or cocoa.

45 mins, plus chilling

45–60 mins

Serves 4

Ingredients

- 1¼ cups heavy cream
- small bunch of mint, chopped
- ½ cup milk
- 6oz (175g) milk chocolate, broken into small pieces
- 3 egg yolks
- 1tbsp confectioners' sugar, plus extra for dusting
- cocoa powder, for dusting (optional)

Equipment

- cutting board
- sharp knife
- 2 saucepans
- mixing bowl
- wooden spoon
- whisk
- sieve
- roasting pan
- 4 ramekins
- cardboard, pencil, scissors

Preheat the oven to 300°F (150°C). Pour the cream into a small pan, then add the mint. Heat gently until nearly boiling, then remove from heat, cover, and let stand for 30 minutes.

Meanwhile, pour the milk into another small pan and heat gently. Remove from the heat and stir in the chocolate pieces until melted and the mixture is smooth.

Whisk the egg yolks and sugar together and add the chocolatey milk and the minty cream. Mix well, then strain the mixture through a fine sieve to remove the mint.

Pour the mixture into 4 ramekins that have been placed in a roasting pan. Add hot water until it's halfway up the outside of the cups. Bake for 45–60 minutes. Let cool, then refrigerate for a few hours. Decorate just before serving.

Stencils

Make a stencil out of cardboard—stars, circles, and flowers work well—and sift confectioners' sugar or cocoa powder on top for a knockout decoration.

Meringue crowns

These beautiful desserts make a great impression.
And the good news is that they are easier to make than they look!
Each crown is large and serves two people, so invite your friends
around to share in the sweetness.

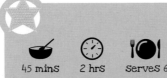

45 mins   2 hrs   Serves 6

For the filling

- ²⁄₃ cup heavy cream, whipped (optional)
- 1 nectarine
- 1 mango
- 1 kiwi

Ingredients

- 3 eggs
- ²⁄₃ cup sugar
- a pinch of salt

Equipment

- baking sheet
- parchment paper
- large bowl
- electric mixer
- tablespoon
- metal mixing spoon
- piping bag
- oven mitts
- cutting board
- sharp knife
- large mixing bowl

1

Line a baking sheet with parchment paper and ask an adult to preheat the oven to 225°F (110°C). Separate the egg whites from the yolks.

2

Beat the egg whites and salt in a large bowl using an electric mixer until they form stiff peaks.

Berry-tastic

You can put any type of fruit into the meringue's center. Try a berry medley of blueberries, raspberries, and strawberries.

3

When the egg whites are stiff, whisk 5 tablespoons of the measured sugar into the mixture, 1 tablespoon at a time. Then fold the remaining sugar into the mixture, using a metal spoon.

4

Draw 3 circles of 4in (10cm) diameter (a saucer works well) onto the parchment paper. Using a piping bag, squeeze the mixture in a spiral. Pipe small peaks to create a crown. Three meringues fit on a sheet.

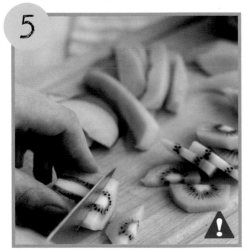

5

Toward the end of the meringue's baking time—on the bottom rack for 2 hours—whip the cream until firm, if using. Carefully slice your fruit, then fill the center of each crown.

10 mins | 1 hr 30 mins | Makes 15

Ingredients

- 2 large egg whites
- ½ cup sugar
- 2 tsp cocoa powder, plus extra for dusting
- ½ cup heavy cream
- 1 tsp peppermint extract (optional)
- 1–2 drops green food coloring (optional)
- 2oz (50g) milk or dark chocolate chips

Equipment

- 2 large baking sheets
- parchment paper
- large mixing bowl
- electric mixer or whisk
- metal tablespoon
- sieve
- teaspoon
- oven mitts

1

Preheat the oven to 275°F (140°C). Grease 2 large baking sheets and line with parchment paper. Beat the egg whites in a bowl until they form stiff peaks.

2

Add the sugar to the egg whites a tablespoon at a time, beating well with the electric mixer or whisk after each spoonful. The mixture should be smooth, thick, and glossy.

3

Sift the cocoa powder over the egg white and sugar mixture. Use a metal tablespoon to fold it over a few times until the mixture is streaked.

4

Using a teaspoon, place heaps of the mixture onto the prepared baking sheets, spaced a little apart, until you have 30 meringues. Flatten each slightly with the back of the spoon.

5

Bake in the preheated oven for 1½ hours, or until the meringues peel away from the parchment paper without resistance. Let them cool on the baking sheets.

6

Whisk the cream, coloring and peppermint extract until thick. Stir in the chocolate chips. Spread the mixture on half of the meringues and sandwich with the other halves. Dust with cocoa.

Cocoa mint meringues

These delicious, cocoa-dusted meringues will melt in your mouth—they're crisp on the outside and soft in the middle! They are filled with lightly whipped peppermint cream and chocolate chips.

Lemon meringue

This family favorite has a crunchy pie crust layered with a tangy lemon filling and a soft meringue topping. It's a taste sensation!

Preheat the oven to 375°F (190°C). Roll out the pastry with a rolling pin on a lightly floured surface to about 10in (25cm). Line the pie pan with the pie dough and chill for 15 minutes.

Prick the pie crust bottom with a fork, line with parchment paper and fill with baking beans or scrunched-up foil. Place on a baking sheet and bake for 15 minutes.

Remove the paper and beans from the pie crust and return to the oven for another 5 minutes, until golden brown. Reduce the oven temperature to 300°F (150°C).

10 mins 55 mins Serves 6

Ingredients

- 6oz (175g) store-bought pie dough
- 3 tbsp cornstarch
- ½ cup cold water
- 2 large lemons
- ⅓ cup sugar
- 2 tbsp butter
- 2 large egg yolks

For the topping

- 2 large egg whites
- ½ cup sugar

Equipment

- rolling pin
- 8in (20cm) round, loose-bottomed fluted pie pan
- fork
- parchment paper
- baking beans or aluminum foil
- baking sheet
- oven mitts
- medium saucepan
- grater
- sharp knife
- cutting board
- pitcher
- wooden spoon
- large mixing bowl
- electric mixer or whisk
- tablespoon
- heatproof bowl

Mix the cornstarch and water together in the saucepan. Grate the zest from the lemons, then cut them in half and squeeze the juice into a pitcher, until you have ¼ cup.

Add the lemon zest and juice to the saucepan, then slowly bring to a boil, stirring continuously with a wooden spoon. Simmer, still stirring, until the mixture thickens.

Remove the saucepan from the heat and stir in the sugar and butter. Let the mixture cool slightly, then beat in the egg yolks. Pour the mixture into the pie crust.

In a clean mixing bowl, beat the egg whites with an electric mixer or whisk until they form stiff peaks. Then beat in the sugar 1 tablespoon at a time, until the mixture is thick and glossy.

Spoon the meringue mixture over the lemon mixture, leaving the rim of the pie crust uncovered. Make peaks in the meringue with the back of the spoon, if you like.

Place the pie on the top rack of the oven and bake for 30–35 minutes, or until the meringue is crisp and golden brown. Serve cold or warm with whipped cream or ice cream.

Raspberry crème brûlée

This traditional French dessert is fun to make and eat. Crème brûlée means "burned cream" and it gets its name from the burned (caramelized) sugar on top.

10 mins, 30 mins Serves 6
plus setting time

Ingredients

- 7oz (200g) fresh raspberries
- 4 large egg yolks
- 5 tbsp superfine sugar
- 2¼ cups heavy cream
- 1 tsp vanilla extract

Equipment

- 6 ramekins
- electric mixer
- soup spoon
- teaspoon
- small saucepan
- baking sheet
- wooden spoon

1

Divide the raspberries equally among the ramekins. Whisk the egg yolks and two tablespoons of sugar in a bowl until pale and creamy.

2

Heat the cream gently (don't boil) for 5 minutes. Remove from the heat, stir in the vanilla, and let cool for 5 minutes. Slowly add the warm cream to the egg mixture, beating constantly.

3

Pour the mixture back into the pan and cook over low heat (do not boil) for a few minutes, stirring constantly. If overheated, the custard will curdle. Pour the custard into the ramekins and let cool.

4

Transfer to the refrigerator to set for 2 hours. Sprinkle the custards evenly with the remaining sugar. Place under a preheated broiler until the sugar bubbles and browns. Let the topping harden for 20 minutes before serving.

Variation

Use ripe peaches or sweet cherries instead of the raspberries for an alternative flavor.

Rhubarb cobblers

A cobbler is a cooked fruit dessert with a topping that resembles a scone or a dumpling. Often, it's made in one large dish, but this recipe is for four individual cobblers.

1 hour, plus sitting time | 25–30 mins | Serves 4

Ingredients

- 12oz (350g) rhubarb, cut into ¾in (2cm) pieces
- grated rind of 1 orange
- ⅓ cup brown sugar
- 1 tbsp cornstarch
- 1¼ cups self-rising flour
- 4 tbsp butter, cut into cubes
- ¼ cup sugar, plus a little for sprinkling
- ½ cup milk, plus extra for brushing

Equipment

- sharp knife
- mixing bowls
- wooden spoon
- round pastry cutter
- 4 ramekins
- pastry brush

1 **Preheat the oven** to 350°F (180°C). Put the rhubarb, orange rind, sugar, and cornstarch in a bowl and stir together. Let the fruit sit for 10–15 minutes.

2 **Meanwhile, make the topping:** put the flour in a large bowl, then add the butter. Use your fingertips to rub the butter into the flour until the mixture looks like fine bread crumbs.

3 **Stir in the sugar,** then add the milk, a little at a time, until you have a slightly sticky, soft dough.

4 **Transfer the dough** to a lightly floured surface and pat it out until it is ½in (1cm) thick. Cut the dough into 8 rounds.

5 **Divide the rhubarb** between 4 ovenproof dishes. Put 2 rounds on top of each. Brush with milk and sprinkle with sugar. Cook on a baking sheet for 25–30 minutes, until golden.

CAKES AND MUFFINS

Savory muffins

Cheese and zucchini give these savory muffins a tasty flavor. They make a great midmorning snack, or pack one in a school lunch!

Tip

To make spinach and cheese muffins, replace the grated zucchini with 6oz (180g) chopped baby spinach leaves in step 3.

10 mins   25 mins   Makes 12

Ingredients

- 2 medium-sized zucchini
- 4oz (125g) mature hard cheese (such as Cheddar)
- 2 cups all-purpose flour
- 1 tbsp baking powder
- 1 tbsp sugar
- 1 tsp salt
- ½ tsp ground black pepper
- 2 eggs, beaten
- ⅔ cup milk
- 6 tbsp lightly salted butter, melted

Equipment

- 2 x 6-hole or 12-hole muffin pan
- 12 paper liners
- grater
- large mixing bowl
- sieve
- metal spoon
- pitcher
- fork or whisk
- oven mitts
- cooling rack

1

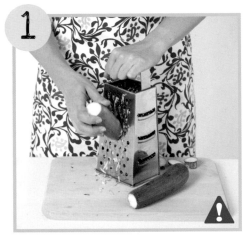

Preheat the oven to 375°F (190°C). Line a muffin pan with 12 paper liners. Trim the ends off the zucchini and grate them coarsely. Grate the cheese.

2

In a large mixing bowl, sift together the flour and baking powder. Stir in the sugar, salt, and pepper with a metal spoon until they are thoroughly combined.

3

Add most of the grated cheese (but save a little to sprinkle on top) and grated zucchini. Using the metal spoon, mix well to combine all the ingredients.

4

In a pitcher, whisk the eggs, milk, and butter with a fork or whisk. Pour them into the large mixing bowl and stir until just combined. The batter should be lumpy.

5

Using the metal spoon, divide the mixture equally among the 12 paper liners and sprinkle each one with the remaining grated cheese.

6

Place the muffins in the center of the oven and bake for 20–25 minutes, until risen, golden, and firm. Let cool on a cooling rack before serving them warm or cold.

Herby cheese muffins

45 mins

20-25 mins

Makes 10

Ingredients

- 2 cups all-purpose flour
- 1 tbsp baking powder
- 1 tsp salt
- 1 tsp mustard powder
- 4½oz (125g) mature Cheddar cheese, grated
- 2 tbsp chopped fresh parsley
- 1 tbsp chopped fresh oregano
- 2 tsp chopped fresh thyme
- freshly ground black pepper
- 2 eggs
- ¾ cup low-fat milk
- 5 tbsp butter, melted

Equipment

- muffin pan
- paper liners
- sieve
- mixing bowls
- sharp knife
- cutting board
- cheese grater
- fork
- wooden spoon

Here is a herby muffin recipe that uses parsley, oregano, and thyme. The muffins are irresistible and best eaten the day they're made, although they will last for a few days if you store them in an airtight container.

Preheat the oven to 375°F (190°C). Line a muffin pan with 10 paper liners. Then sift the flour, baking powder, and salt into a bowl.

Add the mustard, three-quarters of the cheese, and the parsley, oregano, and thyme. Season with black pepper and mix everything together.

In another bowl, beat together the eggs, milk, and melted butter, and pour over the dry ingredients.

Stir the mixture until everything is just combined. Your batter should be very lumpy.

5

⚠️

Spoon the batter into the paper liners, then sprinkle the rest of the cheese on top. Bake for 20–25 minutes, until risen and firm.

Variation

To make basil and tomato muffins, simply follow the main recipe, but swap the herbs for 2 tbsp chopped fresh basil, and stir in 2½oz (75g) chopped sun-dried tomatoes.

Ingredients

- 1 cup all-purpose flour
- 2 tsp baking powder
- ½ tsp baking soda
- ⅓ cup light brown sugar
- ½ cup roasted hazelnuts, chopped
- 3½oz (100g) carrot, grated
- ¾ cup unsulfured apricots, finely chopped
- 1 tbsp poppy seeds
- ½ tsp ground cinnamon
- 1 cup rolled oats
- zest of 2 oranges
- ¾ cup buttermilk, or milk and 1 tbsp lemon juice
- 1 egg, beaten
- 3 tbsp melted butter
- a pinch of salt
- juice of 1 large orange

For the topping

- 2 tbsp brown sugar
- ½ cup rolled oats
- 1 tbsp melted butter

Equipment

- small glass bowl
- baking sheet
- cutting board
- sharp knife
- large glass bowl
- spoon
- paper liners
- muffin pan

Carrot and orange muffins

The versatile carrot can be savory or sweet, as in these delicious muffins—a perfect snack or lunchbox treat.

Preheat the oven to 400°F (200°C). To make the topping, mix together the ingredients in a bowl. Sprinkle the mixture onto a baking sheet. Bake for 5 minutes, then let cool.

In a large bowl, mix the flour, baking powder, baking soda, and sugar. Then add the nuts, carrot, apricots, poppy seeds, cinnamon, oats, and orange zest. Mix together well.

In another bowl, use a spoon to mix the buttermilk, egg, butter, salt, and orange juice. Pour this liquid mixture onto the bowl of dry ingredients.

Stir the two mixtures together using a spoon. Be careful not to overmix, since this will "knock out" all the air. In fact, the lumpier the mixture, the better the muffins will be!

5

Place 8 paper liners in a muffin pan. Spoon the mixture into the liners, filling them two-thirds full.

6

Sprinkle the crumbly topping over the muffins. Bake in the preheated oven for about 25–30 minutes, until well risen and golden brown. Let cool.

Mini muffins

These bite-sized treats have the delicious combination of tasty banana and melt-in-your-mouth chocolate chips. They are perfect for lunchboxes or for a light snack.

10 mins   12 mins   Makes 48

Ingredients

- 2 cups all-purpose flour
- 1 tbsp baking powder
- ½ tsp salt
- ½ cup sugar
- 2 large ripe bananas, peeled and coarsely chopped
- 1 large egg
- 1 cup milk
- 6 tbsp butter, melted
- 6oz (175g) milk chocolate chips or chunks

Equipment

- 24-hole mini-muffin pan
- mini-muffin paper liners (optional)
- large mixing bowl
- sieve
- wooden spoon
- small mixing bowl
- fork
- small whisk
- pitcher
- teaspoon
- oven mitts

1

Preheat the oven to 400°F (200°C). Grease a 24-hole mini-muffin pan with butter (or line it with mini-muffin paper liners) to prevent the muffins from sticking.

2

In a large mixing bowl, sift together the flour, baking powder, and salt. Stir in the sugar with a wooden spoon until all the ingredients are thoroughly combined.

3

In a small mixing bowl, mash the bananas with a fork until nearly smooth, but with a few lumps remaining—this will give the muffins a nice texture.

4

In a pitcher, whisk together the egg, milk, and butter, then pour onto the mashed banana in the bowl. Stir the ingredients until they are well combined.

5

Add the egg and banana mixture to the flour mixture. Stir the ingredients together with a wooden spoon to just combine, then fold in the chocolate chips or chunks.

6

Spoon the mixture into the pan and bake for 10–12 minutes. Let the muffins cool in the pan, then remove them and repeat with the remaining ingredients to make a second batch.

Variation

For variety, use white chocolate chips or chunks in step 5 instead of milk chocolate chips. You can also experiment with other flavors of chocolate.

Cupcakes

Bake these pretty cupcakes and decorate them with pastel-colored icings, candies, or crystallized flowers. Stack in a tower as an alternative way to celebrate a birthday party or baby shower.

Tip

These cupcakes can be made the day before and stored in an airtight container.

· 1¼ cups self-rising flour
· 3 eggs, whisked
· ½ tsp pure vanilla extract

· 2–3 tbsp hot water
· 3 different food colorings
· edible crystallized flowers, sugar strands, sprinkles, and candies

· 2 mixing bowls
· wooden spoon
· 2 metal spoons
· cooling rack
· knife
· 3 small mixing bowls

Ingredients
· 11 tbsp unsalted butter, softened
· ⅔ cup sugar

For the icing and decoration
· 1¾ cups confectioners' sugar, sifted

Equipment
· 2 x 12-hole muffin pans
· 20 paper liners

1

Preheat the oven to 350°F (180°C). Line two 12-hole muffin pans with 20 paper liners.

2

Place the butter, sugar, self-rising flour, eggs, and vanilla extract in a bowl and beat with a wooden spoon until pale and creamy.

3

Divide between the paper liners. Bake for 15 minutes, until golden and just firm. Cool in the pan for 5 minutes, then transfer to a cooling rack to cool.

4

Carefully trim any pointed tops to make a flat surface. Put the cupcakes to one side.

5

Place the confectioners' sugar in a large bowl. Gradually beat in enough water to produce a smooth thick icing that coats the back of a spoon.

6

Transfer the icing mixture to 3 individual bowls and add a few drops of food coloring to each. Spoon onto the cupcakes and top with decorations. Let set.

191

Lime and coconut cupcakes

Give classic cupcakes a makeover with mouthwatering coconut and refreshing lime.

10 mins   20 mins   Makes 18

Ingredients

- 8 tbsp butter, softened
- ½ cup sugar
- finely grated zest and juice of 2 limes
- 2 eggs
- 1 cup self-rising flour
- 1 tsp baking powder
- 1 cup sweetened, dried coconut
- finely grated zest and juice of 1 lime
- 1½ cups confectioners' sugar
- a few drops of green coloring (optional)
- 2 tbsp sweetened, dried coconut

Equipment

- 12-hole muffin pan
- 6-hole muffin pan
- 18 paper liners
- large mixing bowl
- electric mixer or whisk
- metal spoon
- oven mitts
- cooling rack
- small mixing bowl
- sieve
- teaspoon

1

Preheat the oven to 350°F (180°C). Line the muffin pans with 18 paper liners. Use two 12-hole muffin pans if you don't have a 6-hole pan, or bake in batches.

2

In a large mixing bowl, whisk the butter, sugar, and lime zest together using an electric mixer or whisk until they are light and fluffy. Whisk in the eggs and lime juice.

3

Using a metal spoon, fold the flour, baking powder, and coconut into the butter and sugar mixture. Divide the mixture between the paper liners. They should be about two-thirds full.

4

Bake the cupcakes in the oven for 15–20 minutes, until risen and golden brown (bake them on the top rack if you are baking in batches). Transfer to a cooling rack and let cool.

Place two-thirds of the lime zest (saving some for decoration) and lime juice in a bowl and sift over the confectioners' sugar. Stir until smooth, adding a little green food coloring, if using.

Use a teaspoon to drizzle the icing over the tops of the cooled cupcakes and sprinkle over the coconut. Add the saved curls of lime zest to decorate.

Variation

Instead of lime zest and juice, add 2 tsp pure vanilla extract in step 2. Stir a little vanilla extract and water in Step 5 instead of lime zest and juice.

10 mins   20 mins   Makes 18

Carrot cupcakes

The grated carrots make these individual cupcakes perfectly moist, while the yummy cream-cheese frosting adds a deliciously tangy topping.

Ingredients

- 12 tbsp butter, softened
- ⅔ cup sugar
- 1¼ cups self-rising flour
- 2 tsp pumpkin pie spice
- 2 large eggs
- grated zest of 1 orange and 1 tbsp juice
- 2 medium carrots, peeled and coarsely grated
- ½ cup brazil or walnuts, toasted and chopped (optional)

For the frosting

- 7oz (200g) light cream cheese
- 2 tbsp confectioners' sugar
- 1 tbsp orange juice
- 2 tsp grated orange zest

Equipment

- muffin pan
- 18 paper liners
- large mixing bowl
- electric mixer or whisk
- sieve
- soup spoon
- oven mitts
- cooling rack
- wooden spoon
- medium bowl

Preheat the oven to 350°F (180°C). Place 18 paper liners in a muffin pan. Most muffin pans have only 12 holes, so you may have to use 2 pans or cook your cupcakes in batches.

In a large mixing bowl, beat together the butter and sugar until they become pale and fluffy. Use an electric mixer if you have one. If not, use a handheld whisk.

Sift the flour and pumpkin pie spice into the bowl. Then add the eggs, orange juice, and zest. Beat together until all the ingredients are completely combined.

Stir the grated carrots and nuts, if using, into the mixing bowl. Divide the mixture equally between the 18 paper liners using a soup spoon.

5

Bake for 18–20 minutes

in the middle of the oven, until risen
and golden brown. Remove from the
oven using the oven mitts, and place
on a cooling rack to cool completely.

6

Beat together all the frosting

ingredients with a wooden spoon.
Spread the frosting over the cooled
cupcakes and decorate the cupcakes
with extra orange zest.

Banana Squares

The melt-in-your mouth texture of this cake is thanks to the creaming and folding and the buttermilk or yogurt, which make the mixture light and airy. Adding the fresh banana in step 3 also makes the cake deliciously moist.

Ingredients

- 8 tbsp unsalted butter, softened, plus extra for greasing
- ½ cup light brown sugar
- 2 eggs, beaten
- 1½ cups self-rising flour
- a pinch of salt
- 1 tsp baking powder
- 1lb (500g) ripe bananas, peeled and mashed
- 2 tbsp buttermilk or natural yogurt

For the topping

- 1 cup dried coconut
- 7oz (200g) cream cheese, at room temperature
- ½ cup confectioners' sugar, sifted

Equipment

- 8in (20cm) square cake pan
- pencil
- nonstick parchment paper
- scissors
- 2 large mixing bowls
- electric mixer
- sieve
- wooden spoon
- palette knife
- oven mitts
- medium frying pan
- wooden spatula
- plate
- cooling rack

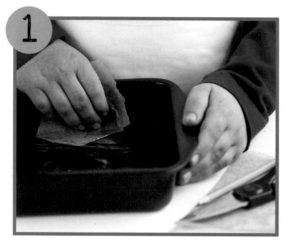

1

Preheat the oven to 350°F (180°C). Draw around the pan onto the parchment paper using a pencil. Cut out the square. Grease and line the pan.

2

Cream the butter and sugar together in a large bowl until light and fluffy. Gradually beat the eggs into the creamed butter and sugar mixture.

3

Sift the flour, salt, and baking powder into the creamed mixture and gently fold them in. Next, stir in the banana and buttermilk.

4

Spoon the cake mixture into the prepared pan and smooth the top with a palette knife. Bake the cake in the oven for 35 minutes, or until firm.

Meanwhile, dry fry

the coconut over low heat until golden brown, stirring continuously. Pour the toasted coconut onto a plate to stop it from burning.

Beat the cheese and

confectioners' sugar together with a wooden spoon until completely combined. It should become smooth, soft, and spreadable.

When the cake is completely

cool, cut it into squares. Add a spoonful of the cream cheese topping and a sprinkling of toasted coconut to each square.

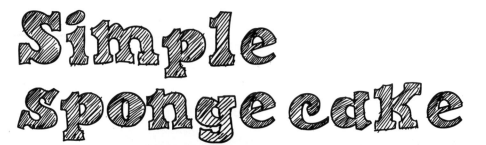

Simple sponge cake

This cake is wonderfully light and moist. You can also make cupcakes with this recipe— see the variation for instructions.

Variation

This mixture will also make 20 cupcakes. Simply divide the mixture between paper liners and bake for 15 minutes.

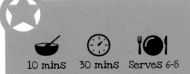

10 mins   30 mins   Serves 6-8

Ingredients

- 12 tbsp butter, softened
- ²/₃ cup sugar
- 3 eggs, beaten
- 1 tsp pure vanilla extract

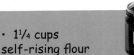

- 1¼ cups self-rising flour
- 1 tsp baking powder
- 4 tbsp raspberry or strawberry jam
- confectioners' sugar, for dusting

For the buttercream

- 4 tbsp butter, softened
- 1 cup confectioners' sugar
- ½ tsp vanilla extract
- 2 tsp milk

Equipment

- 2 x 8in (20cm) round cake pans
- parchment paper

- large mixing bowl
- sieve
- electric mixer or whisk
- soup spoon
- oven mitts
- cooling rack
- mixing bowl
- wooden spoon
- spatula

1

Preheat the oven to 350°F (180°C). Grease two 8in (20cm) round cake pans and line each with parchment paper so that the sponge cakes don't stick.

2

Place the butter, sugar, eggs, and vanilla extract in a large bowl and sift over the flour and baking powder. Using an electric mixer or whisk, beat all the ingredients together until thick.

3

Divide the mixture between the two pans, leveling the tops with the back of a soup spoon. Bake in the center of the oven for 25–30 minutes, or until risen and firm to the touch.

4

Let the cakes cool in the pans for a few minutes, then turn them onto a cooling rack. Peel off the parchment paper and let the cakes cool completely.

5

To make the buttercream, place the butter, confectioners' sugar, vanilla extract, and milk in a mixing bowl. Beat them together with a wooden spoon until smooth and creamy.

6

Spread the flat side of one of the cakes with the jam. Spread the flat side of the other with the buttercream, then sandwich the two halves together. Dust with confectioners' sugar.

Variation

When strawberries aren't in season—or if you want to try something different—use 6oz (175g) of peaches or apricots from a can. Make sure you drain the peaches or apricots from the juices that they are preserved in.

Strawberry cake

Make this delicious cake for a family party or a friend's birthday. You'll have lots of fun filling it with strawberries and decorating it with confectioners' sugar.

Preheat the oven to 350°F (180°C). Line the pans with parchment paper. Mix the butter and sugar with an electric mixer until light and creamy.

Beat in the eggs a little at a time, then sift in the flour and fold it in gently with a metal spoon.

Divide the mixture between the pans and bake for 25 minutes. Cool briefly in the pans, then turn onto a wire rack to cool.

Beat the cream in a bowl. Put the strawberries and cream on one cake. Place the other cake on top. Dust thickly with confectioners' sugar.

20 mins   25 mins   Serves 10

Ingredients
- 16 tbsp butter, at room temperature
- 1 cup sugar
- 4 large eggs, lightly beaten
- 2 cups self-rising flour
- confectioners' sugar, for dusting

For the filling:
- ½ cup heavy cream
- 6oz (175g) strawberries, hulled and sliced

Equipment
- 2 x 8in (20cm) round cake pans
- electric mixer
- parchment paper

Lemon and lime cake

The lemon and lime juice make this cake scrumptiously moist and full of flavor, while the runny glaze icing adds an extra sweetness. You family and friends will love it!

15 mins | 60 mins | Serves 12

Ingredients
- 12 tbsp butter, at room temperature
- ²/₃ cup sugar
- 3 large eggs, lightly beaten
- grated zest of 1 lemon
- grated zest of 1 lime
- 2 tbsp lemon juice
- 1¼ cups self-rising flour
- 2 tbsp poppy seeds (optional)
- 1 tbsp lime juice
- ¾ cup confectioners' sugar

Equipment
- electric mixer
- large mixing bowl
- loaf pan
- parchment paper
- sieve
- spatula
- cooling rack
- small mixing bowl
- spoon

Preheat the oven to 350°F (180°C). Using an electric mixer, beat the butter and sugar until light and fluffy. Line the loaf pan with parchment paper.

Beat in the eggs a little at a time, then gently fold in the lemon and lime zest, together with one tablespoon of the lemon juice. Sift in the flour, then fold in with the poppy seeds, if using.

Transfer to the pan and smooth the top. Bake for one hour, or until golden brown. Cool in the pan for 5 minutes, then move to a wire rack.

Mix the remaining lemon juice with the lime juice. Sift in the confectioners' sugar and combine to make a runny icing. Spoon it on the cake.

Tip

A sprinkling of
poppy seeds adds
a finishing touch
to your cake.

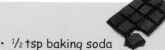

35 mins 30 mins Serves 12

Ingredients

- 12 tbsp butter, softened
- 1 cup brown sugar
- 1 cup self-rising flour
- ¼ cup cocoa powder
- 1 tsp baking powder
- ½ tsp baking soda
- 3 eggs, beaten
- ½ cup sour cream

For the frosting

- 6oz (175g) white chocolate, broken into small pieces
- 8 tbsp butter
- 4 tbsp milk
- 1²/₃ cups confectioners' sugar
- grated chocolate, chocolate buttons, and cocoa powder, for dusting (optional)

Equipment

- 2 x 8in (20cm) cake pans
- parchment paper
- 2 large mixing bowls
- electric mixer or whisk
- sieve
- spatula
- oven mitts
- cooling rack
- heatproof bowl
- saucepan
- wooden spoon
- palette knife

Preheat the oven to 325°F (170°C). Grease and line the bottom of the pans with parchment paper. Place the butter and sugar in a mixing bowl and beat together until combined.

Sift over the flour, cocoa powder, baking powder, and baking soda. Add the eggs and sour cream and beat with an electric mixer or whisk until well combined.

Divide the mixture between the two pans and level the tops. Bake for 25–30 minutes. Let cool slightly, then turn onto a cooling rack. Remove the parchment paper.

Make the frosting. Place the milk, chocolate, and butter in a heatproof bowl over a saucepan of simmering water. Stir occasionally until the ingredients are melted and smooth.

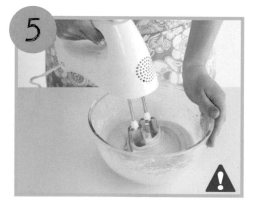

Sift the confectioners' sugar into a bowl, then pour over the melted chocolate mixture. Beat together with the whisk. Let the frosting cool, then beat again until it forms soft peaks.

Use a little of the frosting to sandwich the two cakes together. Spread the remaining frosting over the top and sides of the cake. Decorate as desired and dust with cocoa powder.

Double chocolate fudge cake

If you are a chocolate lover, you will adore this cake!
The dark chocolate sponge cake is filled and topped with a white
chocolate frosting.

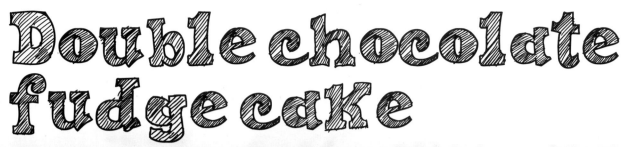

Jelly roll

Deliciously light sponge cake is combined with fruity jam in this classic dessert. The technique can be tricky to master, so you might need help from an adult.

15 mins   10 mins   Serves 8

Ingredients

- 1 tbsp vegetable oil
- 3 large eggs
- ½ cup sugar, plus extra for dusting
- ¾ cup self-rising flour

For the filling

- 5 tbsp raspberry jam

Equipment

- 13 x 9in (33 x 23cm) pan
- pastry brush
- parchment paper
- large mixing bowl
- electric mixer
- sieve
- metal spoon
- oven mitts
- clean damp dish towel
- sharp knife
- palette knife

1

Preheat the oven to 400°F (200°C). Brush the bottom and sides of a 13 x 9in (33 x 23cm) pan with a little vegetable oil, then line with parchment paper. Brush with a little more oil.

2

Beat the eggs and sugar together in a bowl, using an electric mixer. Beat for about 10 minutes until the mixture is light and frothy and the beaters leave a trail when lifted.

3

Sift the flour into the mixture, carefully folding at the same time with a metal spoon. Pour the mixture into the prepared pan and shake it gently so that the mixture is level.

4

Place the filled pan on the top rack of the oven. Bake for about 10 minutes, or until the sponge cake is golden brown and begins to shrink from the edges of the pan.

5

Lay a damp dish towel on the work surface. Place a piece of parchment paper a little bigger than the size of the pan onto the dish towel and sprinkle it with sugar.

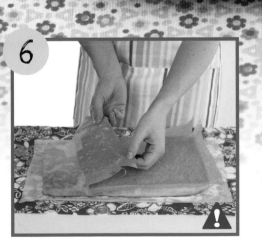

6

Using oven mitts, turn the warm cake onto the sugared paper so it is upside down. Take off the mitts and gently loosen the parchment paper and peel it off.

7

Trim the edges of the cake with a sharp knife. Make a score mark 1in (2.5cm) from one shorter edge, being careful not to cut all the way through. This makes the cake easier to roll.

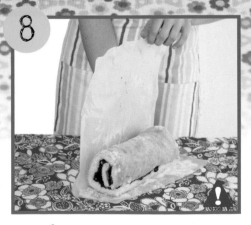

8

Let the sponge cake cool a bit, then spread the jam over it with a palette knife. Roll up firmly from the cut end. Place the roll on a plate seam-side down. Serve in slices.

Lemon drizzle cake

It would be hard to find a more lemony cake than this one. The luscious lemon sponge has a contrasting crusty top made by pouring the lemon syrup over the cake while it is still warm.

 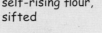

20 mins   40 mins   Serves 8

Ingredients

- finely grated zest of 2 organic lemons
- 14 tbsp butter, softened
- ¾ cup sugar
- 3 eggs, beaten
- 1½ cups self-rising flour, sifted
- syrup
- juice 4 lemons (about ½ cup)
- ⅓ cup granulated sugar

Equipment

- 8in (20cm) round springform cake pan
- parchment paper
- large mixing bowl
- electric mixer or whisk
- metal spoon

- oven mitts
- small mixing bowl
- toothpick
- cooling rack

1

Preheat the oven to 350°F (180°C). Butter an 8in (20cm) round, springform cake pan and line the bottom with parchment paper to prevent the cake from sticking to the pan.

2

Place the lemon zest, butter, and sugar in a large mixing bowl and beat until the mixture is light and fluffy. You can use an electric mixer or whisk.

3

Beat in the eggs a little at a time. If the mixture starts to curdle, add 1 tablespoon of the flour. Use a metal spoon to fold in the flour, then spoon the mixture into the prepared pan.

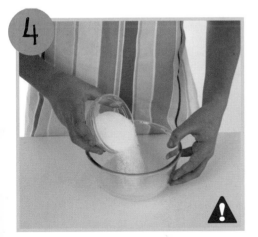

4

Bake the cake in the center of the oven for 35–40 minutes. Put the lemon juice and granulated sugar in a small bowl. Leave in a warm place, stirring occasionally.

5

When the cake has risen, and is golden and shrinking from the pan, remove it from the oven and prick all over with a toothpick about 20 times.

6

Drizzle the juice over the cake slowly. It will leave a crust as it sinks in. Let the cake cool in the pan for 10 minutes, then carefully transfer it to a cooling rack.

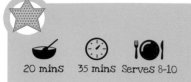

20 mins　35 mins　Serves 8-10

Ingredients

- 8 tbsp butter, softened
- ½ cup sugar
- 2 large eggs
- ½ cup milk
- ½ tsp baking soda
- 1¼ cups self-rising flour

For the topping

- 2 apples
- 4 tbsp butter, diced
- ⅓ cup light brown sugar

- 1 tsp ground cinnamon (optional)

Equipment

- 8in (20cm) round cake pan with sides 3in (7.5cm) deep
- peeler
- corer
- sharp knife
- cutting board
- small mixing bowl
- spoon
- large mixing bowl
- electric mixer or whisk
- sieve
- spatula
- oven mitts

1

Preheat the oven to 350°F (180°C). Grease the bottom and sides of an 8in (20cm) round cake pan, 3in (7.5cm) deep. The cake pan should not be a springform or loose-bottomed pan.

2

Peel the apples with a peeler, then use a corer to remove the cores from the centers. Cut each apple into 5 rings and place in the bottom of the pan, overlapping if necessary.

3

In a small mixing bowl, mix together the butter, sugar, and cinnamon, if using, and sprinkle the mixture over the apple rings in the bottom of the cake pan.

4

Place the butter and sugar in a large bowl. Using an electric mixer or whisk, beat them together until pale and fluffy. Beat in the eggs, adding a little flour if the mixture starts to curdle.

5

Beat in the milk and baking soda a little at a time, along with some of the flour. Sift over the remaining flour and stir the mixture together until they are just combined.

6

Pour the cake mixture over the apple rings and spread evenly, using a spatula. Bake the cake in the center of the oven for 30–35 minutes, until golden brown and firm to the touch.

Upside-down apple cake

This fruity cake is fun to make and impressive to look at!
Rings look prettier, but slices of apple or pineapple also work.

7

Cool the cake in the pan for 5 minutes, then turn it out. Serve the apple upside-down cake in slices. It can be eaten cold or warm with custard, whipped cream, or ice cream.

Banana and buttermilk cake

This cake has a lovely crumbly texture that combines nicely with crunchy nuts and soft gooey banana. It is a great way to use up ripe bananas.

15 mins | 1 hr | Serves 10

Ingredients

- 3 ripe bananas, broken into pieces
- 1 tsp lemon juice
- 1 cup pecan halves (optional)
- 7 tbsp butter, softened
- 1 cup brown sugar
- 2 eggs, beaten
- 1 tsp pure vanilla extract
- 2 cups all-purpose flour
- 1 tsp salt
- 1 tsp baking soda
- 1 tsp pumpkin pie spice
- ½ cup buttermilk
- 1 small banana, sliced

Equipment

- 9 x 5in (23 x 12cm) loaf pan
- parchment paper
- 2 small bowls
- fork
- large mixing bowl
- electric mixer or whisk
- sieve
- metal spoon
- aluminum foil
- cooling rack

Preheat the oven to 350°F (180°C). Grease and line the bottom of a 9 x 5in (23 x 12cm) loaf pan with parchment paper. Use a fork to mash the banana pieces with the lemon juice.

Use your hands to break the pecan halves into small pieces in a bowl if you are adding nuts. If you don't like nuts, just omit this step.

Place the butter and sugar in a large mixing bowl. Using an electric mixer or whisk, beat them together until they are combined and become light and fluffy.

Beat in the eggs and vanilla extract, a little at a time. Stir in the banana mixture. Sift in the flour, salt, baking soda, and pumpkin pie spice and stir into the mixture with a metal spoon.

212

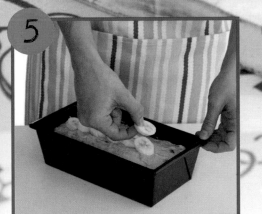

5 **Stir in the buttermilk.** Add the nuts, if using, saving a few. Pour the mixture into the pan and place the sliced banana on the top. Sprinkle over the saved nuts.

6 **Bake in the oven** for 50–60 minutes. If the cake becomes too brown, cover it with foil. Let the cake cool in the pan, then turn it onto a cooling rack and remove the parchment paper.

Variation

Replace the pecans with chopped walnuts or brazil nuts, or just omit them.

Marble cake

Chocolate and orange cake batters are swirled together to create a spectacular marble effect. This cake is lots of fun to make, and you can change your swirling patterns every time you make it! Serve it cold or hot, with ice cream or whipped cream. Delicious!

10 mins   30 mins   Makes 25

Ingredients

- 12 tbsp butter, softened
- $\frac{2}{3}$ cup sugar
- $1\frac{1}{4}$ cups self-rising flour
- 3 large eggs
- grated zest of 1 orange
- 2 tbsp orange juice
- 2 tbsp cocoa powder

Equipment

- 8in (20cm) square cake pan
- parchment paper
- large mixing bowl
- electric mixer or whisk
- large spoon
- sieve
- butter knife
- oven mitts
- cutting board
- sharp knife

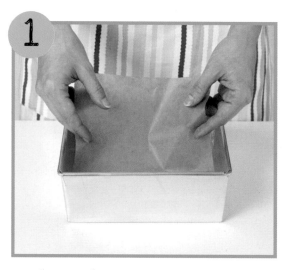

1

Preheat the oven to 350°F (180°C). Grease and line the bottom of an 8in (20cm) square cake pan with parchment paper to prevent the cake from sticking.

2

Put all the ingredients except the cocoa powder in a large mixing bowl. Using an electric mixer or handheld whisk, beat them together until smooth.

3

Divide the batter in half. Place large spoonfuls of one half of the batter into the pan in each of the 4 corners and in the middle. Leave space between each spoonful.

4

Sift the cocoa powder over the remaining batter in the bowl and beat together until combined. Spoon the chocolate batter into the spaces in the cake pan.

Gently drag a butter knife through the batters to create a swirl effect with the brown and white batters. Don't overdo it, or you will mix the colors together completely.

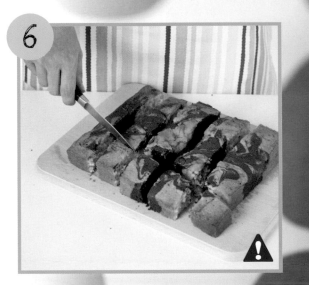

Bake the cake for 30 minutes, until risen and springy. Let it cool in the pan, then remove it and peel off the parchment paper. Cut the cake into 25 squares with a sharp knife.

Blueberry and sour cream cake

Adding sour cream makes this pretty cake wonderfully moist and creamy. It can be decorated with fresh blueberries for an extra burst of fruity flavor!

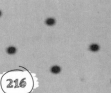

25 mins 50 mins Serves 10

Ingredients

- 6 tbsp butter, softened
- 1 cup sugar
- 1 cup sour cream
- 2 eggs

- 2 tsp pure vanilla extract
- 2½ cups self-rising flour
- 1 tsp baking powder
- 8oz (225g) blueberries

For the frosting

- 7oz (200g) cream cheese
- finely grated zest of 1 lemon

- 1 tsp pure vanilla extract
- 1 tbsp lemon juice
- ¾ cup confectioners' sugar
- 4oz (125g) blueberries

Equipment

- 9in (23cm) round springform cake pan
- parchment paper

- 2 large mixing bowls
- electric mixer or whisk
- sieve
- metal spoon
- cooling rack
- small bowl
- wooden spoon
- oven mitts
- palette knife

1

Preheat the oven to 350°F (180°C). Grease a 9in (23cm) round springform cake pan and line the bottom with parchment paper to prevent the cake from sticking.

2

Place the butter and sugar in a large mixing bowl. Using an electric mixer or whisk, cream the butter and sugar together until they are light and fluffy.

3

Whisk in a little of the sour cream until the batter is smooth. Beat in the remaining sour cream, eggs, and vanilla extract until thoroughly combined and smooth.

4

Sift the flour and baking powder over the batter and gently fold together using a metal spoon. Gently fold in the blueberries, then spoon the batter into the pan. Level the top.

5

Bake for 45–50 minutes or until the cake feels firm. Let the cake cool in the pan for 10 minutes, then turn onto a cooling rack and peel off the paper. Let cool completely.

6

Beat the cream cheese, lemon zest, and juice with a wooden spoon in a bowl. Sift over the confectioners' sugar and beat in. Spread the frosting on the cake and decorate with blueberries.

Tropical fruitcake

This cake is deceptively simple to make. The pineapple and mango add a tropical flavor, but you can use any of your favorite dried fruit. Serve the fruitcake warm or cold—it tastes great either way.

15 mins   1 hr   Serves 12

Ingredients

- 1²/₃ cups mixed, dried tropical fruit, e.g., pineapple, mango, papaya, apricots
- ³/₄ cup raisins
- 1 tsp pumpkin pie spice
- 8 tbsp butter, diced
- ½ cup brown sugar
- ½ cup cold water
- 1½ cups self-rising flour
- 1 egg, beaten

Equipment

- 2lb (900g) loaf pan
- parchment paper or loaf pan liner
- cutting board
- sharp knife
- medium saucepan
- wooden spoon
- skewer
- oven mitts

Grease and line the bottom of a 2lb (900g) loaf pan, or use a loaf pan liner. On a cutting board, carefully cut the tropical fruit into small pieces with a sharp knife.

Place the raisins, dried tropical fruit, pumpkin pie spice, butter, sugar, and water in a medium saucepan. Warm over low heat until the butter has melted, stirring with a wooden spoon.

Bring the butter and fruit mixture to a boil and let simmer for 5 minutes. Remove the saucepan from the heat and let the mixture cool completely.

Preheat the oven to 300°F (150°C). When the mixture is cool, stir in the flour and the egg with the wooden spoon until combined. Spoon the mixture into the prepared pan.

Bake in the center of the oven for 50–60 minutes, or until a skewer inserted into the middle comes out clean. Let the cake cool in the pan. When cool, serve in slices.

Variation

For a different take on this recipe, replace the tropical fruits with currants, golden raisins, more raisins, and candied cherries.

Ingredients

- 7oz (200g) graham crackers
- 4 tbsp butter
- 20oz (600g) cream cheese
- ½ cup sour cream
- ¼ cup cornstarch
- ⅔ cup confectioners' sugar, sifted
- 3 eggs
- 1 tsp pure vanilla extract
- 8oz (225g) fresh raspberries

To Serve

- fresh raspberries
- confectioners' sugar, for dusting

Equipment

- food bag
- rolling pin or food processor
- cutting board
- wooden spoon
- saucepan
- 8in (20cm) round springform cake pan
- large mixing bowl
- electric mixer or whisk
- metal spoon
- baking sheet
- oven mitts

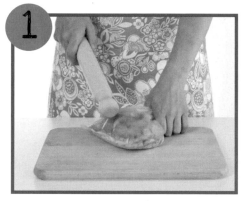

1

Preheat oven to 325°F (170°C). Place the graham crackers in a food bag and crush them with a rolling pin. You can also do this in a food processor.

2

Melt the butter in a saucepan and stir in the crushed graham crackers. Press the mixture into the bottom of the pan with the back of a spoon. Chill in the fridge for 15 minutes.

3

Place the cream cheese and sour cream in a large mixing bowl. Using an electric mixer or handheld whisk, beat the mixture until smooth. Then beat in the cornstarch and confectioners' sugar.

4

Add the eggs and vanilla extract to the bowl and whisk until smooth. Using a metal spoon, carefully stir in the raspberries. Pour this mixture over the cracker crust.

5

Place the cake on a baking sheet and bake for 35–40 minutes in the middle of the oven until just set. Let it cool, then chill the cake in the fridge for 2–3 hours, or overnight.

6

Carefully remove the cake from the springform pan and decorate with the fresh raspberries. Dust the cheesecake with confectioners' sugar, then serve it in slices.

Baked raspberry cheesecake

This baked cheesecake is so simple to make. You can replace the raspberries with blueberries for a different taste. Serve it at a party for friends or family—they'll love it.

COOKIES
AND
BARS

Star cookies

These cookies make great gifts for the holidays. You can use different-shaped cookie cutters for different themes, such as Christmas, Halloween, or Valentine's Day.

25 mins   50 mins   Serves 10

Ingredients

- 1½ cups all-purpose flour
- 8 tbsp butter, diced
- ½ cup sugar
- 1 tsp ground cinnamon
- finely grated zest of 1 orange
- 1 egg, lightly beaten
- 2 tbsp maple syrup or honey

To decorate

- ribbon, royal icing, edible silver balls or sprinkles

Equipment

- 2 large baking sheets
- parchment paper
- food processor
- small bowl
- fork
- rolling pin
- star-shaped cutter
- bamboo skewer
- oven mitts
- cooling rack

1

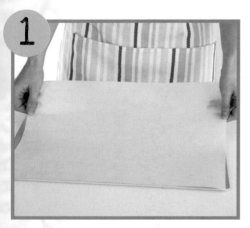

Preheat the oven to 350°F (180°C). Line 2 large baking sheets with parchment paper. Pulse the flour and butter in a food processor, until the mixture resembles fine bread crumbs.

2

Add the sugar, cinnamon, and orange zest and pulse again. In a small bowl, beat together the egg and maple syrup or honey with a fork, then add this to the bread crumb mixture.

3

Process the mixture in the food processor until it comes together in a ball. Lift out the ball of dough, wrap it in plastic wrap and chill for 10 minutes in the fridge.

4

Roll out the chilled dough on a lightly floured surface, to ¼in (4–5mm) thickness. Cut into stars using a shaped cookie cutter. Reroll and cut out more stars until you use up all the dough.

5

Place the stars slightly apart on the baking sheets and bake for 10–12 minutes. Let cool for 2 minutes. If they are being used as decorations, poke a hole in the top of each using the skewer.

6

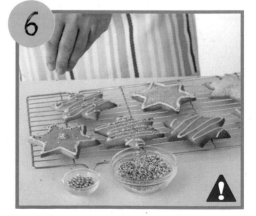

Transfer the stars to a cooling rack. When they are cool, decorate them as desired. Thread the holes with ribbon and tie the ends together if you are using them as decorations.

Raisin cookies

These simply scrumptious cookies are sure to become a favorite. They are perfect for an afternoon snack or a light dessert.

20 mins   14 mins   Makes 20

Ingredients
- 8 tbsp butter, softened
- ⅓ cup sugar
- finely grated zest of 1 lemon
- 1 egg, separated
- 1½ cups all-purpose flour,   sifted
- ½ cup raisins
- 2 tbsp milk
- 1–2 tbsp sugar, for sprinkling

Equipment
- 2 large baking sheets
- large mixing bowl
- electric mixer or whisk
- butter knife
- rolling pin
- 2½in (6cm) round fluted pastry cutter
- oven mitts
- fork
- pastry brush
- palette knife
- cooling rack

Preheat the oven to 350°F (180°C). Grease 2 baking sheets. In a bowl, beat the butter, sugar, and lemon zest together using an electric mixer or whisk until they are pale and fluffy.

Beat in the egg yolk but keep the egg white to one side. Using a butter knife, gently stir in the sifted flour and raisins. Gradually stir in the milk until the dough comes together.

Turn the dough onto a lightly floured surface and knead it gently until it is smooth and supple. Shape the dough into a ball with your hands.

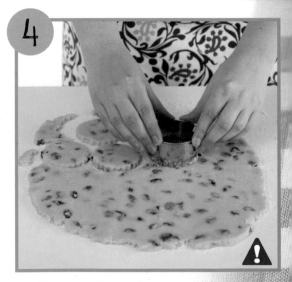

Roll the dough out to about ¼in (5mm) thick, then cut out the cookies using a 2½in (6cm) round fluted cookie cutter. Place the cookies on the baking sheets and bake for 8–10 minutes.

5

Using oven mitts, remove the baking sheets from the oven. Lightly whisk the egg white with a fork, then brush it over the cookies with a pastry brush and sprinkle them with sugar.

6

Wearing the oven mitts, return the cookies to the oven for 3–4 minutes, until they turn golden. Once baked, remove the cookies from the oven and transfer them to a cooling rack.

Variation

Replace the raisins with currants or golden raisins if you like, or spice things up by adding a little cinnamon or pumpkin pie spice.

Tip

A good way to measure maple syrup or honey is to lightly grease the tablespoon with a little oil. You'll find the syrup or honey will run off the spoon into the pan.

Coconut cookies

Give oat cookies a tasty tropical twist by adding creamy coconut. The baking soda gives the cookies a great crunchy texture.

10 mins   10 mins   Makes 20

Ingredients

- 1 cup dried coconut
- ¾ cup all-purpose flour
- ½ cup sugar
- 1¼ cups rolled oats
- 7 tbsp butter, diced
- 1 tbsp maple syrup or honey
- 1 tsp baking soda
- 2 tbsp hot water

Equipment

- 2 baking sheets
- parchment paper
- large mixing bowl
- wooden spoon
- medium saucepan
- soup spoon
- oven mitts
- palette knife
- cooling rack

1

Preheat the oven to 350°F (180°C). Line 2 baking sheets with parchment paper. Place the coconut, flour, sugar, and oats in a mixing bowl and mix together with a wooden spoon.

2

Place the butter and maple syrup or honey in a medium saucepan and heat over low heat until melted. Stir the mixture with a wooden spoon to mix thoroughly.

3

Mix the baking soda with the hot water. Add it to the butter mixture in the saucepan. The baking soda will make the butter and syrup or honey mixture fizz. Stir well.

4

Pour the butter mixture into the large mixing bowl and mix well. Spoon the mixture onto the baking sheets with a soup spoon, leaving room between each one for the cookies to spread.

5

Bake the cookies for 8–10 minutes on the top rack of the oven until golden brown. Let the cookies cool on the sheet for 5 minutes, then transfer to a cooling rack to cool completely.

229

Jam shapes

These pretty jam-filled cookies take time to make, but they are definitely worth the effort! The combination of gooey jam and crunchy cookie is heavenly.

15 mins, plus chilling   15 mins   Makes 18

Ingredients

- 12 tbsp butter, softened
- ²⁄₃ cup sugar
- 1 tsp pure vanilla extract
- 1 tsp finely grated lemon zest
- 1 egg, beaten
- 1 egg yolk
- 2 cups all-purpose flour, plus extra for rolling out
- 6 tbsp raspberry or strawberry jam
- 2 tbsp confectioners' sugar, for dusting

Equipment

- 2 large baking sheets
- parchment paper
- food processor
- plastic wrap
- rolling pin
- 2½in (6cm) cookie cutter
- 1–1½in (2–3cm) cookie cutter
- oven mitts
- cooling rack
- palette knife

Preheat the oven to 325°F (170°C). Line 2 baking sheets with parchment paper. Process the butter, sugar, vanilla extract, and lemon zest in a food processor until smooth.

Add the egg, egg yolk, and flour to the food processor and process again, until the mixture resembles bread crumbs and is starting to come together in a dough.

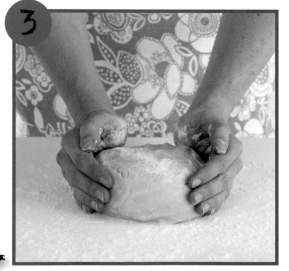

Transfer the dough to a lightly floured surface and lightly knead until it is smooth. Flatten into a circle, wrap it in plastic wrap, and chill for 30 minutes.

On a lightly floured surface, roll out the dough to ¼in (3mm) thick. Using a 2½in (6cm) cookie cutter, cut out as many cookies as you can. You should get about 36 in total.

5

Use a 1–1½in (2–3cm) cookie cutter to cut out the middle from 18 of the cookies; you can bake these too if you like. Arrange on the baking sheets and chill for 15 minutes.

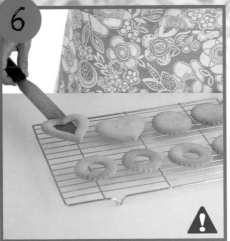

6

Bake on the center rack of the oven for about 10–12 minutes, or until golden brown. Bake in batches, if necessary. Cool them on the baking sheets for 1 minute, then transfer to a cooling rack.

7

When completely cool, spread the whole cookies with jam. Dust confectioners' sugar on the cookies with holes. Press one sugar-dusted cookie onto each jam-covered one and serve.

15 mins 10 mins Makes 15

Ingredients

- 2½ cups all-purpose flour
- 2 tsp ground ginger
- 1 tsp baking soda
- 8 tbsp butter, diced
- ¾ cup dark brown sugar
- ¼ cup maple syrup or honey
- 1 egg, beaten
- candies, raisins, and royal icing for decoration

Equipment

- 2 large baking sheets
- parchment paper
- large mixing bowl
- wooden spoon
- rolling pin
- cookie cutters of your choice
- oven mitts

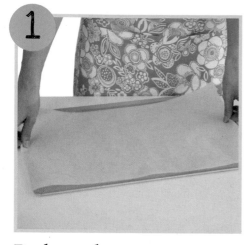

Preheat the oven to 350°F (180°C). Line 2 large baking sheets with parchment paper. If you only have 1 baking sheet, you will need to bake the cookies in 2 batches.

Place the flour, ginger, and baking soda in a large bowl. Stir the ingredients together with a wooden spoon until they are thoroughly combined.

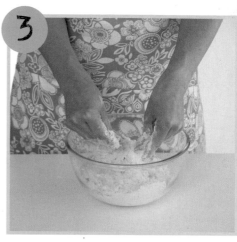

Rub the butter into the mixture using your fingertips. Continue rubbing in the butter until the mixture resembles fine bread crumbs. Stir in the sugar.

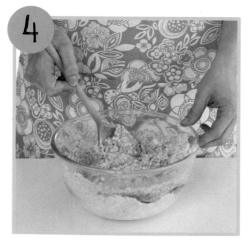

Stir in the syrup or honey and egg until the mixture starts to come together in a dough. Turn the dough mixture onto a lightly floured surface and knead it until smooth.

Roll out the dough on a lightly floured surface to a thickness of ¼in (5mm). Using your cookie cutters, cut out the shapes. Reroll the leftover dough and cut out more cookies.

Place the cookies on the baking sheets and bake for 9–10 minutes. Let the cookies cool on the sheets. Decorate with candies, raisins, and royal icing.

Gingerbread

Gingerbread tastes great and smells wonderful as it bakes. This recipe can be used for round cookies, pretty tree decorations, or gingerbread people

Melting moments

These melt-in-your-mouth cookies are a chocolate-lover's dream! The creamy filling and crunchy cookie make a tasty combination.

20 mins · 15 mins · Makes 15

- ¼ cup cornstarch
- ¼ cup cocoa powder, sifted

Ingredients

- 12 tbsp butter, softened
- ¼ cup sugar
- 1 tsp pure vanilla extract
- ¾ cup all-purpose flour

For the filling

- 3½oz (100g) good quality chocolate, broken into pieces
- 2 tbsp heavy cream

Equipment

- 2 large baking sheets
- parchment paper
- large mixing bowl
- electric mixer or wooden spoon
- sieve
- metal spoon
- teaspoon
- oven mitts
- cooling rack
- palette knife
- heatproof bowl
- small saucepan
- wooden spoon

1

Preheat the oven to 350°F (180°C). Line 2 baking sheets with parchment paper. Place the butter, sugar, and vanilla extract in a bowl and beat with an electric mixer or wooden spoon.

2

Sift the all-purpose flour, cornstarch, and cocoa powder into the mixing bowl. Using a metal spoon, fold them into the mixture until the ingredients are well combined.

3

Using a teaspoon, spoon 15 x 1in (2.5cm) dollops onto each baking sheet so you have 30 in total. Leave room between each one because they will spread while baking.

4

Bake for 12–15 minutes, or until they are just starting to become dark around the edges. Remove them from the oven and let cool slightly before moving to a cooling rack.

5

Place the chocolate and cream in a heatproof bowl over a saucepan of simmering water. Stir them until they have melted. Remove from the heat and let cool completely.

6

Spread the filling on the flat side of half of the cooled cookies with a palette knife and sandwich each one with one of the remaining cookies.

Orange oatmeal cookies

These oaty cookies are flavored with tangy orange. The sunflower seeds are a great source of vitamins and minerals, plus they add that delicious extra crunch!

15 mins   10 mins   Makes 14

Ingredients

- 1½ cups rolled oats
- ¾ cup sunflower seeds
- ¾ cup self-rising flour
- 10 tbsp butter, diced
- finely grated zest of 1 orange
- 2 tbsp orange juice
- ¾ cup light brown sugar
- 2 tbsp maple syrup or honey

Equipment

- 3 large baking sheets
- parchment paper
- large mixing bowl
- wooden spoon
- medium saucepan
- soup spoon
- oven mitts
- cooling rack
- palette knife

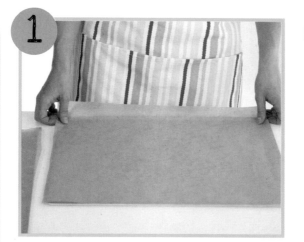

Preheat the oven to 350°F (180°C). Line 3 large baking sheets with parchment paper to prevent the cookies from sticking to them.

Place the oats, sunflower seeds, and flour in a large mixing bowl. Stir the mixture with a wooden spoon until completely combined. Set the bowl to one side.

Place the butter, orange zest, juice, sugar, and syrup or honey in a medium saucepan. Heat the mixture over low heat while stirring, until the butter and sugar have melted.

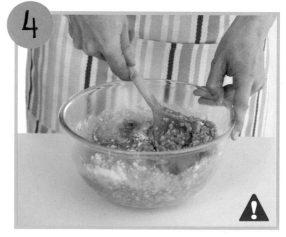

Carefully pour the butter mixture over the ingredients in the large mixing bowl and mix them together with the wooden spoon until thoroughly combined.

5

Place heaping spoonfuls of the cookie dough onto each sheet. Leave a generous space between each cookie, since they will spread. Bake for 8–10 minutes, until the cookies are golden.

6

Let the cookies cool on the baking sheet for a few minutes, then transfer them to a cooling rack with a palette knife, to become crisp. They will keep in an airtight container for 2–3 days.

Tip

To make smaller cookies, place heaping teaspoons instead of soup spoons of the mixture on the baking sheets and bake for 7–9 minutes.

Four ways with cookies

Making cookies is fun, and eating them is even more fun! Try these tasty combinations or come up with your own.

Basic cookie dough

This recipe is for 8 people (which allows for 2 cookies each). It takes 40 mins to prepare (including chilling time) and 15 mins to bake.

- 7 tbsp butter, at room temperature
- 1 egg
- ½ cup sugar
- ½ tsp pure vanilla extract
- 1 cup self-rising flour

Equipment

- 2 baking sheets
- parchment paper
- large glass bowl
- electric mixer
- wooden spoon

1

Hazelnut delights

Hazelnuts have a wonderful flavor and crunchy texture. If you want, you can use the same quantity of another nut. Do you like peanuts, walnuts, pecans, or pistachios?

Ingredients

(to add to basic dough recipe above)

- ⅔ cup hazelnuts, cut in half

Top tips

- Roast the nuts under the broiler for 2 minutes before you stir them into the dough.

- Wrap a stack of cookies in parchment paper and tie it with ribbon to make a package to give as a gift.

2

Cranberry chews

You can play around with the recipe by using the same quantity of another dried fruit. Which is your favorite? Try raisins, mangoes, apples, blueberries, or cherries.

Ingredients

(to add to basic dough recipe above)

- 1½oz (45g) white chocolate, broken into small pieces

- ¼ cup dried cranberries, finely chopped

Top tips

- Mix the ingredients well so that the cranberries and white chocolate don't all sit together. They need to be spread out within each cookie.

- Serve the cookies with a glass of milk for each person.

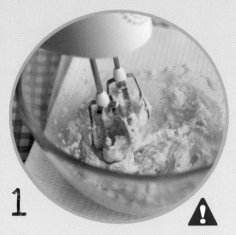

1

Preheat the oven to 350°F (180°C). Line 2 sheets with parchment paper. In a large bowl, use an electric mixer to beat the butter and egg together. Mix in the sugar and vanilla.

2

Work in the flour with a spoon until the mixture forms a soft dough, then mix in your additional ingredients from one of the recipes below. Chill in the fridge for 30 minutes.

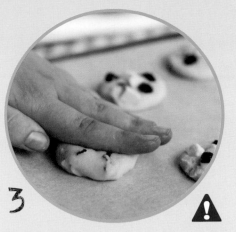

3

Roll the dough into about 16 balls and place on the baking sheets, leaving space around each ball. Flatten the balls slightly and bake in the oven for 15 minutes, or until golden. Cool on a wire rack.

3

Classic chocolate chip

This traditional cookie is one that everyone likes. For variety, use milk chocolate chunks or white chocolate chunks. Nuts add a twist to this cookie recipe.

Ingredients

(to add to dough recipe above)

· 2¹/₂oz (75g) dark chocolate, broken into small pieces

Top tips

• Make the chunks fairly big so that they are nice and gooey when you bite into a cookie.

• On a cold day, make hot chocolate to serve with the cookies for a real chocolatey treat.

4

Apricots and cinnamon

Try other spices in place of cinnamon. Substitute the same amount of pumpkin pie spice for the cinnamon or add half that amount of ground ginger. You can use raisins or golden raisins instead of apricots.

Ingredients

(to add to basic dough recipe above)

· 2¹/₂oz (75g) dried apricots, finely chopped

· ¹/₄ tsp ground cinnamon

Top tips

• Make the apricot pieces small so that they are scattered throughout each cookie.

• Store in a cookie jar for a couple of days, if they don't get eaten before then!

Chocolate cookies

This is a versatile recipe for melt-in-your-mouth cookies. You can use either chocolate spread for a double chocolate taste or peanut butter for a nutty flavor.

35 mins   40 mins   Makes 20

Ingredients

- 8 tbsp unsalted butter, softened
- 1½ cups all-purpose flour
- ½ cup light brown sugar
- 1 egg
- ⅓ cup sugar
- ½ tsp baking powder
- ¼ cup cocoa powder
- ½ cup chocolate spread
- 2-3 drops pure vanilla extract
- 1 pinch of salt
- 5oz (150g) white chocolate chips

Equipment

- 2 mixing bowls
- electric mixer
- sieve
- wooden spoon
- plastic spatula
- soup spoon
- teaspoon
- 3 baking sheets
- oven mitts
- palette knife
- cooling rack

Preheat the oven to 350°F (180°C). Cream the butter and both types of sugar together in a large bowl until the mixture turns creamy.

Still using the electric mixer, beat the egg, chocolate spread, and vanilla extract into the creamed butter and sugar mixture, until fully combined.

Sift the flour, baking powder, cocoa powder, and salt into a bowl. Use a wooden spoon to push the mixture through, if you need to.

Add the sifted flour mixture to the chocolate mixture and gently mix them together with a wooden spoon. Stir in the chocolate chips.

5

Place 6–7 heaping
spoonfuls of the cookie dough onto each baking sheet, leaving space between each mound so they can spread as they bake.

6

Bake for 14 minutes.
Take the sheets out of the oven and let the cookies set for 2–3 minutes. When set, transfer them to a cooling rack.

Variation

For a nutty cookie, omit the cocoa powder in step 3, swap the chocolate spread for the same amount of peanut butter in step 2, and use dark chocolate chips instead.

Tip

Milk or dark chocolate would also taste great in these cookies. If you prefer other dried fruits, such as strawberries or blueberries, use them instead of cranberries.

Chocolate and cranberry cookies

The perfect combination of tart cranberries and sweet white chocolate makes these cookies melt in your mouth!

10 mins · 15 mins · Makes 15

Ingredients

- 8 tbsp butter, softened
- ¾ cup light brown sugar
- 1 egg, beaten
- 1 tbsp milk
- 1 cup all-purpose flour
- ½ tsp baking powder
- 2oz (50g) white chocolate, finely grated
- 3½oz (100g) white chocolate chips
- ½ cup dried cranberries

Equipment

- 2 baking sheets
- parchment paper
- large mixing bowl
- electric mixer or whisk
- soup spoon
- cooling rack
- spatula

1

Preheat the oven to 375°F (180°C). Line 2 baking sheets with parchment paper to prevent the cookies from sticking while they are baking.

2

Cream the butter and sugar in a large bowl until they are pale and creamy. Use an electric mixer or whisk. Beat in the egg and milk.

3

Add the flour, baking powder, grated chocolate, chocolate chips, and cranberries to the mixture. Using a soup spoon, stir until they are thoroughly combined.

4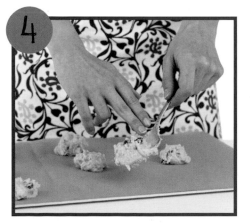

Place spoonfuls of the cookie dough onto the prepared baking sheets. Leave space between the spoonfuls so the cookies do not merge together as they bake.

5

Bake for 12–15 minutes, until lightly golden and slightly soft to the touch. Let cool on the sheet for 5 minutes, then transfer to a cooling rack to cool completely.

Rocky road cookies

These gorgeous cookies are topped with chunky chocolate and melted marshmallows. The chunky and smooth textures are a perfect combination. Yum!

10 mins   11 mins   Makes 14

Ingredients

- 8 tbsp butter, softened
- ¾ cup brown sugar
- 1 egg, beaten
- 1 tbsp milk
- 2oz (50g) milk chocolate, chopped
- ¾ cup all-purpose flour
- 1 tbsp cocoa powder
- ½ tsp baking powder
- 2oz (50g) white chocolate, chopped
- 1oz (25g) mini marshmallows

Equipment

- 2 baking sheets
- parchment paper
- large mixing bowl
- electric mixer or whisk
- metal spoon
- soup spoon
- oven mitts
- palette knife
- cooling rack

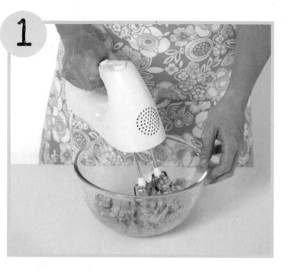

1

Preheat the oven to 375°F (180°C). Line 2 baking sheets with parchment paper. Use an electric mixer or whisk to cream the butter and sugar together in a mixing bowl.

2

Beat in the egg and milk. Use a metal spoon to stir in the flour, cocoa powder, baking powder, and half the chunks of milk and white chocolate.

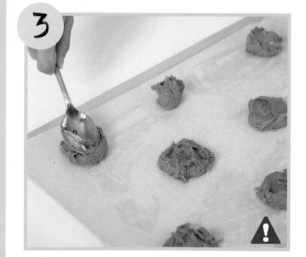

3

Place spoonfuls of the cookie dough onto the prepared baking sheets, spacing them well apart. Flatten slightly and bake for 5 minutes, until the edges are starting to become firm.

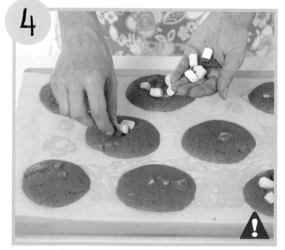

4

Remove the cookies from the oven. Immediately sprinkle the cookies with the marshmallows and remaining chocolate chunks, pressing them down into the cookies.

244

5

Return the cookies

to the oven for another 5–6 minutes, or until slightly soft to the touch. Let them cool for 5 minutes, then transfer to a cooling rack.

Variation

Experiment with different flavored chocolate chunks. Or try heart-shaped marshmallows for a Valentine's Day treat!

Tip

Don't be tempted to take the oat bars out of the pan until they are completely cool, or they will break up.

Oat bars

Tasty crumbly oats mixed with sticky maple syrup and crunchy corn flakes make these oat bars completely irresistible. Oats release energy slowly, so you won't feel hungry for a while after you eat them.

Preheat the oven to 350°F (180°C). In a saucepan, gently melt the butter, sugar, and maple syrup or honey over low heat, stirring with a wooden spoon until the sugar has dissolved.

Remove the saucepan from the heat and gently stir in the oats and corn flakes with the wooden spoon, until the mixture is thoroughly combined and sticky.

10 mins   25 mins   Makes 16

Ingredients

- 12 tbsp butter, diced
- 1 cup light brown sugar
- ¼ cup maple syrup or honey
- 3¾ cups rolled oats
- 1 cup corn flakes

Equipment

- large saucepan
- wooden spoon
- 11 x 7in (28 x 18cm) pan
- oven mitts
- sharp knife

Pour the mixture into an 11 x 7in (28 x 18cm) pan and spread it into the corners. Gently press down with the back of the wooden spoon to make the top flat and even.

Bake the mixture for 25 minutes, or until golden and firm. Let cool for 10 minutes, then cut it into bars. Let cool completely before lifting the bars out of the pan.

Ginger and pumpkin slices

This sticky pumpkin and ginger cake is wonderfully dark and moist. It tastes even better the day after baking—if you can resist it that long!

15 mins   40 mins   Makes 18

Ingredients

- 8 tbsp butter
- ½ cup dark brown sugar
- ⅔ cup maple syrup or honey
- ⅔ cup dark molasses
- 9oz (250g) pumpkin, grated
- 2 cups all-purpose flour
- 1 tsp baking soda
- 2 tsp ground ginger
- 2 eggs, beaten

Equipment

- 9in (23cm) square cake pan
- parchment paper
- medium saucepan
- wooden spoon
- large mixing bowl
- oven mitts
- cutting board
- sharp knife

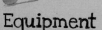

Preheat the oven to 350°F (180°C). Grease the bottom of a 9in (23cm) square cake pan with a pat of butter on some parchment paper. Line the pan with parchment paper.

Place the butter, sugar, maple syrup or honey, and molasses in a medium pan and heat gently until the sugar has dissolved and the butter has melted. Remove from the heat and let cool.

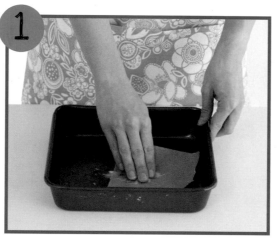

In a large mixing bowl, add the grated pumpkin or butternut squash, flour, baking soda and ginger. Mix thoroughly with a wooden spoon.

Stir in the molasses mixture and beaten eggs until combined, then pour into the greased and lined pan. Bake in the center of the oven for 35–40 minutes, or until firm.

5

Let the cake cool in the pan. Once cool, carefully turn onto a cutting board. Peel the paper off the back and cut the cake into rectangles with a sharp knife.

Variation

If pumpkins are not in season, use grated butternut squash instead. They have a similar flavor because they are both part of the squash family of vegetable.

10 mins   30 mins   Makes 24

Ingredients

- 1 cup pitted dates, coarsely chopped
- ½ cup cold water
- 1 tsp baking soda
- 10 tbsp butter, softened
- ¾ cup light brown sugar
- 2 eggs, beaten
- 1 tsp pure vanilla extract
- 1¼ cups self-rising flour

For the caramel topping

- 6 tbsp caramel sauce (Dulce de Leche)

Equipment

- 11 x 7in (28 x 18cm) baking pan
- parchment paper
- small saucepan
- large mixing bowl
- electric mixer or handheld whisk
- metal spoon
- oven mitts
- cooling rack
- cutting board
- sharp knife
- palette knife

Caramel bars

These caramel treats are yummy!

For extra stickiness, the bars are topped with a caramel sauce. You can buy caramel sauce in a jar, but it's more fun to make your own.

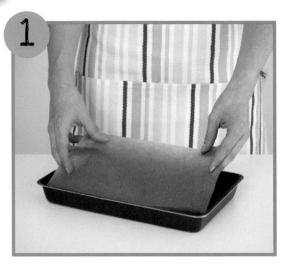

Preheat the oven to 350°F (180°C). Lightly grease an 11 x 7in (28 x 18cm) pan and line the bottom with parchment paper to prevent the cake from sticking.

Place the dates in a pan and add the water. Bring to a boil, then remove from the heat and add the baking soda—the mixture will fizz! Set aside to cool slightly.

Place the butter and sugar in a large mixing bowl. Using an electric mixer or whisk, beat them together until they are light and fluffy. Beat in the eggs and vanilla extract.

Using a metal spoon, fold in the flour, then the date mixture. Pour the mixture into the pan. Place it in the center of the oven and bake for 25–30 minutes, or until risen.

5

Let the cake cool in the pan for 10 minutes, then transfer it to a cooling rack. When cold, cut it into 24 squares, then spread your caramel sauce over the top with a palette knife.

Tip

To make your own caramel sauce, bring 5 tbsp butter, ¾ cup light brown sugar, and ½ cup light cream to a boil and cook for 3 minutes, until thickened. Let cool.

Chocolate fudge brownies

These delicious brownies are perfect—crisp on the outside and fudgy on the inside. Be careful not to overbake them—they should be gooey in the center.

20 mins   25 mins   Makes 36

Ingredients

- 18 tbsp butter
- 10oz (275g) 70% cocoa dark chocolate, broken into pieces
- 1¼ cups sugar
- three large eggs
- 1 tsp pure vanilla extract
- 1½ cups all-purpose flour
- ½ tsp salt

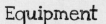

Equipment

- 9in (23cm) square cake pan
- parchment paper
- medium saucepan
- wooden spoon
- large mixing bowl
- electric mixer or whisk
- metal spoon
- oven mitts
- cooling rack
- sharp knife

1

Preheat the oven to 350°F (180°C). Grease and line the bottom of a 9in (23cm) square cake pan with parchment paper to keep the brownies from sticking.

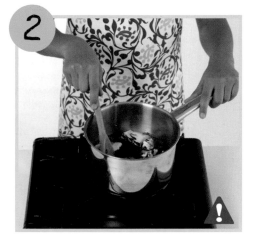

2

Melt the butter and chocolate in a medium saucepan over low heat, stirring occasionally with a wooden spoon. Remove the saucepan from the heat and let cool slightly.

3

In a large mixing bowl, beat together the sugar, eggs, and vanilla extract using an electric mixer or whisk. Keep beating until the mixture is pale and fluffy.

4

Beat the chocolate mixture into the egg mixture until thoroughly combined, using an electric mixer or whisk. Stir in the flour and salt with a metal spoon.

5

Pour the mixture into the prepared pan and bake for 20–25 minutes in the center of the oven, until the brownies are just set. The center should be slightly gooey.

6

Let the cake cool for 10 minutes in the pan. Turn onto a cooling rack. When the brownies are cooled, remove the parchment paper and cut them into squares.

Chocolate & raspberry brownies

These pretty brownies, dotted with fresh raspberries and white chocolate, are delicious—and so easy to make.

15 mins · 40 mins · Makes 16

Ingredients

- 9oz (250g) white chocolate
- 6 tbsp butter
- ½ cup sugar
- 2 large eggs, beaten
- 1 tsp pure vanilla extract
- 1¼ cups all-purpose flour
- ½ tsp salt
- 5oz (150g) fresh raspberries

Equipment

- 8in (20cm) square cake pan
- parchment paper
- 2 medium-sized bowls
- saucepan
- electric mixer
- sieve
- metal spoon
- plastic spatula
- knife

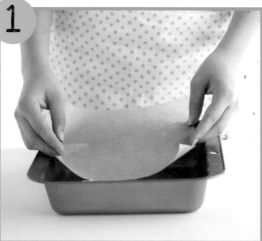

1 **Preheat the oven** to 350°F (180°C). Grease and line the bottom of an 8in (20cm) square cake pan with parchment paper.

2 **Break up the chocolate.** Put 6oz (175g) in a bowl. Set the bowl over a pan of simmering water until the chocolate is melted and smooth. Cool slightly.

3 **Beat the butter** and sugar together until fluffy in a medium bowl. Beat in the eggs and vanilla extract, then stir in the melted chocolate.

4 **Sift the flour** and salt over the mixture and fold in. Then gently fold in the saved broken chocolate and the raspberries.

5

Spoon the mixture into the pan, spread into the corners, then level with a plastic spatula. Cook for 30–35 minutes. Cool before cutting into squares.

Tip

Brownies should be firm on the outside but gooey and fudgelike on the inside.

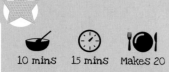

Ingredients

10 mins   15 mins   Makes 20

- 1¾ cups oatbran
- 2oz (50g) Cheddar cheese, finely grated
- ½ tsp salt
- ½ tsp baking soda
- 1 tsp paprika (optional)
- 2 tsp fresh rosemary, chopped (optional)
- 2 tbsp butter, melted
- 1 egg yolk
- ¼ cup warm water

Equipment

- large baking sheet
- large mixing bowl
- wooden spoon
- rolling pin
- 2½in (6cm) cookie cutter
- oven mitts

1

Preheat the oven to 400°F (200°C). Lightly grease a large baking sheet with a pat of butter on a piece of parchment paper to prevent the oatcakes from sticking to the sheet.

2

Place the oatbran, cheese, salt, baking soda, paprika, and rosemary in a large mixing bowl. Stir the ingredients together with a wooden spoon until they are well combined.

3

Stir in the butter, egg yolk, and water to make a sticky dough. Place the dough on a lightly floured surface and use your hands to press the mixture together.

Tip

You can store the oatcakes in an airtight container for up to a week. Don't keep them any longer, or they will start to become soft.

4

Roll out the dough very thinly to about ⅛in (2mm) thick on a lightly floured surface. Using a 2½in (6cm) cookie cutter, cut out the crackers. Gather the trimmings, reroll, and cut out.

5

Place the crackers on the baking sheet. Place the sheet on the top rack of the oven and bake for 15 minutes. Remove the baking sheet from the oven and let the oatcakes cool completely.

Cheesy oatcakes

These crunchy savory crackers are delicious served warm or cold. They are perfect for a snack or a light lunch. Serve them with your favorite cheese and a salad or relish.

Cheesy shortbread

These light and savory shortbreads make a perfect afternoon snack. Or you can serve them as appetizers at a party and watch them disappear!

30 mins, plus chilling — **25 mins** — **Makes 20**

Ingredients

- ³/₄ cup all-purpose flour
- pinch of cayenne pepper
- 7 tbsp butter, diced
- 3oz (75g) Parmesan cheese, freshly grated
- 1 egg yolk
- 1 tsp olive oil

To glaze

- egg yolk, beaten with a little milk
- 1 tsp poppy seeds

Equipment

- large baking sheet
- large mixing bowl
- metal spoon
- butter knife
- plastic wrap
- rolling pin
- 2in (5cm) round cookie cutter
- pastry brush
- oven mitts
- palette knife
- cooling rack

1

Lightly grease a large baking sheet with butter. Preheat the oven to 325°F (170°C). Place the flour and cayenne pepper in a large mixing bowl and mix together with a metal spoon.

2

Add the butter to the flour mixture. Rub it in using your fingertips until the mixture resembles bread crumbs. Stir in the Parmesan cheese with a metal spoon.

3

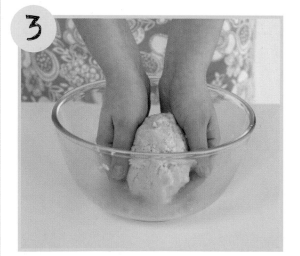

Add the egg yolk and olive oil and stir the mixture together with a butter knife. Using your hands, form the mixture into a ball of dough. Wrap it in plastic wrap and chill for 30 minutes.

4

Using a floured rolling pin, roll out the chilled dough on a lightly floured surface to ½in (5mm) thick. Using a 2in (5cm) round cookie cutter, cut out 16 circles. Put them on the baking sheet.

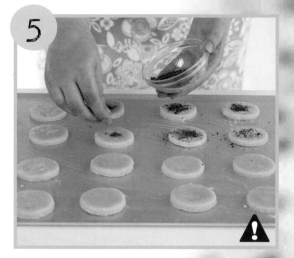

5

Brush the tops of the circles with the egg yolk glaze and then sprinkle them with the poppy seeds. Bake them on the top rack for 20–25 minutes, or until golden.

6

Let the shortbread cookies cool on the baking sheet for a few minutes. Using a palette knife, transfer them to a cooling rack to cool completely.

Basic bread

Making bread is lots of fun, and the smell of baking bread will make your mouth water! This easy basic dough recipe can be made into delicious rolls or a traditional loaf. Replace the bread flour with whole wheat bread flour if you want to make whole wheat bread.

Variation

To make rolls, divide the dough into 8 balls at Step 5. Flatten slightly. Place on a greased baking sheet, cover with a damp dish towel, and let rise for 30 minutes. Brush with milk, then sprinkle seeds on top. Bake for 20–25 minutes.

20 mins, plus rising

30 mins

Makes 1 loaf

Ingredients

- 1½ tsp active dried yeast
- 1 tsp sugar
- 1½ cups lukewarm water
- 3 cups bread flour
- 2 tsp salt

Equipment

- 2lb (900g) loaf pan
- small mixing bowl
- wooden spoon
- sieve
- clean, damp dish towel
- large mixing bowl
- oven mitts
- cooling rack

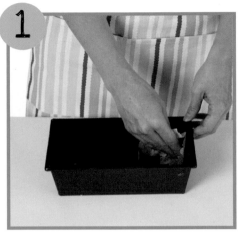

1

Lightly grease a 2lb (900g) loaf pan with butter. Place the yeast, sugar, and a little of the water in a small bowl, stir well, and leave in a warm place for 10 minutes, until frothy.

2

Sift the flour and salt into a large mixing bowl. Make a well in the center and pour in the frothy yeast mixture and remaining water. Stir with a wooden spoon to form a dough.

3

Knead the dough on a lightly floured surface for 10 minutes. Put back in the bowl, cover with a damp dish towel, and leave in a warm place for an hour, or until doubled in size.

4

Preheat the oven to 425°F (220°C). Lightly punch down the dough. This knocks out the large air bubbles. Knead it lightly on a floured surface.

5

Shape the dough into a rectangle and tuck the ends under to fit into the pan. Place in the pan. Cover with the damp dish towel and let rise in a warm place for another 30 minutes.

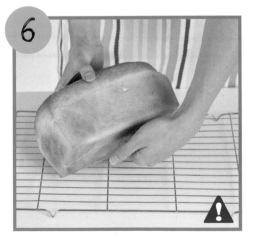

6

Place the pan in the center of the oven. Bake for 30 minutes, or until risen and golden brown. Turn out the loaf and tap the bottom—it should sound hollow. Place on a cooling rack.

Italian bread

This dimpled bread, known as focaccia,

can be flavored with herbs, cheese, sun-dried tomato, or olives. It's so yummy, you'll keep coming back for more!

30 mins, plus rising **25 mins** Serves 6-8

Ingredients

- 2½ cups bread flour
- ¼oz (7g) package fast-acting dried yeast
- ½ tsp salt
- ⅔ cup warm water
- ¼ cup olive oil

To finish

- 1 tbsp olive oil
- coarse sea salt, for sprinkling

Equipment

- sieve
- large mixing bowl
- large metal spoon
- baking sheet
- clean, damp dish towel
- rolling pin
- oven mitts

1

Sift the flour into a large mixing bowl, add the salt, and stir in the yeast with a large metal spoon. Lightly oil a baking sheet to prevent the focaccia from sticking.

2

Make a well in the center of the flour with the large metal spoon. Stir in the warm water and olive oil until the mixture starts to come together to form a smooth dough.

3

Transfer to a lightly floured surface and knead for 10 minutes, until smooth and elastic. Place back in the bowl, cover with a clean, damp dish towel and let rise in a warm place for an hour.

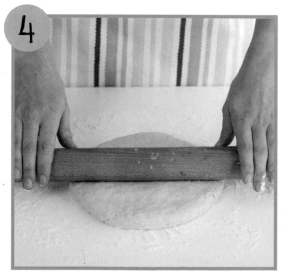

4

Punch down the dough to remove the large air bubbles, then place it on a lightly floured surface. Using a rolling pin, roll out to an 8in (20cm) circle about ⅜in (1cm) thick.

5

Place the rolled-out dough on the oiled baking sheet and cover with a clean, damp dish towel. Leave the dough to rise in a warm place for 30 minutes.

6

Preheat the oven to 400°F (200°C). Using your fingertips, make dimples all over the surface of the risen dough and drizzle with the olive oil.

7

Sprinkle the dough with the sea salt. Place in the oven on the middle rack. Bake for 20–25 minutes, until risen and golden. It's delicious eaten warm!

Flatbreads

These flatbreads taste great served with hummus and dips or with grilled food. They are best eaten as soon as they are made, when they are still soft and warm.

15 mins, plus rising   3 mins   Makes 6

Ingredients

- 2 cups white bread flour
- 1 tsp fast-acting dry yeast
- 1/2 tsp sugar
- 1/2 tsp salt
- 2/3 cup lukewarm water

Equipment

- large mixing bowl
- wooden spoon
- clean, damp dish towel
- rolling pin
- nonstick frying pan
- spatula or palette knife

Place the flour, yeast, sugar, and salt in a large mixing bowl and mix well with a wooden spoon. Make a well in the center and stir in enough of the water to form a soft dough.

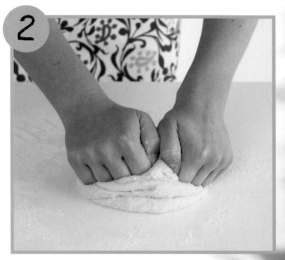

Place the dough on a lightly floured surface and knead for 5 minutes, until smooth and elastic.

Return the dough to the bowl and cover with a clean, damp dish towel. Leave it in a warm place for an hour, or until the dough has doubled in size.

Punch down the dough with your fist to remove the large air bubbles. Next, divide the dough into 6 equal chunks.

5

Knead each chunk lightly on a lightly floured surface to make a flatter round shape. Roll out each piece of dough into a 5in (13cm) circle with a rolling pin.

6

Preheat a frying pan. Add a flat piece of dough and cook for a minute, until golden underneath. Then flip it over and cook the other side for 30 seconds. Serve immediately.

Variation

You can add different ingredients to the flour mixture in step 1, such as 1 tbsp of freshly chopped rosemary, chopped scallions, or crushed garlic.

Sunflower loaves

Fill your kitchen with the homey smell of bread-making. Sunflower seeds are great to nibble on, too, while your bread is baking.

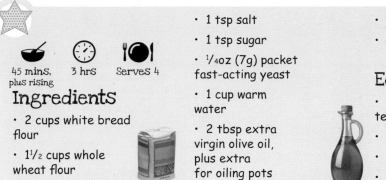

- 45 mins, plus rising
- 3 hrs
- Serves 4

Ingredients

- 2 cups white bread flour
- 1½ cups whole wheat flour
- 1 tsp salt
- 1 tsp sugar
- ¼oz (7g) packet fast-acting yeast
- 1 cup warm water
- 2 tbsp extra virgin olive oil, plus extra for oiling pots
- 1 cup sunflower seeds
- a little milk

Equipment

- 4 x 5 x 4in (11 x 10cm) terra-cotta flowerpots
- liquid measuring cup
- mixing bowl
- baking sheet
- plastic bag
- pastry brush
- wooden spoon

Wash the pots thoroughly. Preheat the oven to 400°F (200°C). Oil the pots inside and out and bake for 35–40 minutes. Let them cool. Repeat the process two more times.

Put the flour, salt, sugar, and yeast into a large bowl. Make a well in the center and pour in the water and olive oil. Mix to make a soft, but firm dough.

Turn the dough onto a lightly dusted work surface and knead well for at least 10 minutes. Ask an adult to take a turn if your arms get tired.

Make a well in the dough and add three-quarters of the sunflower seeds. Knead them into the dough so that they're evenly spread.

Divide the dough into 4 pieces and place one ball into each flowerpot. Cover the pots with a plastic bag and leave until the dough has doubled in size.

Brush the tops of the risen loaves with milk. Sprinkle over the remaining sunflower seeds and bake for 35–40 minutes, or until golden brown. Cool in the pots.

269

10 mins   25 mins   Makes 8

Ingredients

- 4 tbsp butter, diced
- 1 bunch scallions, sliced (optional)
- ¾ cup self-rising flour
- ¾ cup whole wheat flour
- 1 tbsp baking powder
- ½ tsp salt
- 1 tsp mustard powder
- 4oz (125g) mature Cheddar cheese, grated
- 1 large egg
- ½ cup milk
- 1 egg, beaten, or milk, for brushing

Equipment

- baking sheet
- saucepan
- wooden spoon
- large mixing bowl
- sieve
- butter knife
- sharp knife
- pastry brush
- oven mitts
- cutting board

1

Preheat the oven to 400°F (200°C). Lightly grease a baking sheet. Melt 2 tablespoons butter in a saucepan, add the scallions, and cook over medium heat for 2–3 minutes.

2

Sift the flours, baking powder, and salt into a bowl. Use your fingertips to rub the remaining butter into the flour, until the mixture resembles fine bread crumbs.

3

Stir in the mustard powder, two-thirds of the cheese, and the cooked scallions, then mix well. Beat together the egg and milk, then stir them into the flour mixture with a butter knife.

4

Gently knead the dough on a lightly floured surface to remove any cracks. Place the dough on the baking sheet and shape it into a 7in (18cm) round about ¾in (2cm) thick.

5

Using a sharp knife, divide the round into 8 wedges, cutting deeply into the dough. Using a pastry brush, brush the tops with the egg or milk and sprinkle the remaining cheese on top.

6

Cook the round for 20–25 minutes, or until risen and golden. Cover the top with foil if it becomes too brown. Place it on a cutting board and cut into wedges. Serve warm or cold.

Cheese and onion round

This savory scone round makes a delicious accompaniment to soup or salad. It also tastes great on its own spread with a little butter.

Tip

To make sure that the scone round rises well while baking, don't handle the dough too roughly or for too long in step 4.

Multigrain braid

This multigrain braid is fun to make and nutritious. If you want to make a white braid, just use white bread flour instead of the multigrain bread flour.

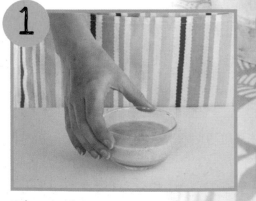

1

Place the yeast, sugar, and a little of the water in a small bowl. Stir well with a teaspoon and leave in a warm place for 10 minutes, until the mixture turns frothy.

2

Place the flour and salt in a large mixing bowl. Rub in the butter with your fingertips until it is thoroughly mixed into the flour.

3

Make a well in the center and pour in the frothy yeast mixture and remaining water. Stir with a wooden spoon to form a dough, then use your hands to form a ball.

15 mins, plus rising | 30 mins | 1 loaf

Ingredients

- 1½ tsp active dried yeast
- 1 tsp sugar
- 1½ cups lukewarm water
- 3 cups multigrain bread flour
- 2 tsp salt
- 2 tbsp butter, diced
- flour, for dusting

Equipment

- small mixing bowl
- teaspoon
- large mixing bowl
- wooden spoon
- clean, damp dish towel
- baking sheet
- knife
- oven mitts

4

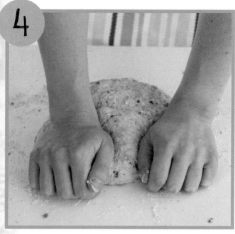

Knead the dough on a lightly floured surface for 10 minutes, until the dough is smooth and elastic.

5

Place the dough in a lightly oiled bowl, cover with a clean, damp dish towel, and let rise in a warm place for an hour, or until it has doubled in size.

6

Preheat the oven to 425°F (220°C). Lightly grease a baking sheet. Place the dough on a lightly floured surface. Punch down the dough to get rid of the air bubbles.

7

Shape the dough into a rectangle, then cut it into three equal pieces. Use your hands to roll each piece of dough into a 12in (30cm) long sausage.

8

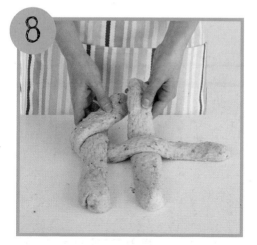

Make an "H" with the dough pieces, weaving the middle piece over the piece on the left and under the piece on the right. Braid from the center downward. Turn the dough around and repeat.

9

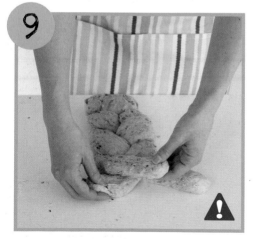

Tuck the ends under and place on the baking sheet. Let rise for nother 30 minutes. Bake for 30 minutes, or until hollow when tapped. Remove from the pan and let cool.

Cornbread

10 mins **30 mins** **Serves 12**

Ingredients

- ¾ cup all-purpose flour
- 1 cup cornmeal or polenta
- 1 tbsp baking powder
- 1 tsp salt
- 5 scallions, thinly sliced (optional)
- 5½oz (150g) canned corn
- 2 eggs
- 1 cup buttermilk or plain yogurt
- ½ cup milk
- 4 tbsp butter, melted and cooled

Equipment

- 8in (20cm) square cake pan or 8in (20cm) ceramic pie dish
- pastry brush
- large mixing bowl
- wooden spoon
- liquid measuring cup
- whisk
- oven mitts
- sharp knife

This cornbread recipe is really simple to make, and the corn and scallions give it an unusual texture.

Preheat the oven to 400°F (200°C). Grease an 8in (20cm) square cake pan or a round 8in (20cm) ceramic pie dish. The recipe works in either a pan or a dish.

In a large mixing bowl, place the flour, cornmeal or polenta, baking powder, salt, chopped scallions, and corn. Mix together thoroughly with a wooden spoon and set aside.

In a liquid measuring cup, whisk together the eggs, buttermilk or yogurt, milk, and melted butter with a small hand whisk until they are thoroughly combined and frothy.

Pour the egg and milk mixture into the flour mixture in the large mixing bowl. Stir with a wooden spoon to combine all the ingredients thoroughly.

5

Pour the mixture into the prepared dish. Bake for 25–30 minutes, until golden brown and beginning to pull away from the sides. Let cool in the pan before cutting into wedges.

Tip

Is the tea loaf baked?
To find out, push a skewer
into the middle. Then pull
it out. If it comes out
clean, the tea loaf
is ready.

Whole wheat tea loaf

Whole wheat flour is an essential ingredient in this fruity, cakelike tea loaf. It's super easy to make and is best eaten while still warm from the oven—either plain or spread with creamy butter.

20 mins   20-25 mins   Serves 8-12

Ingredients

- butter, for greasing
- ½ cup dried mixed fruits, such as raisins, golden raisins, and currants
- ½ cup dried cranberries
- ½ cup warm tea
- 2 tbsp honey
- 1 egg, beaten
- 1¼ cups whole wheat flour
- 1 tbsp baking powder
- ½ tsp pumpkin pie spice

Equipment

- mixing bowl
- wooden spoon
- soup spoon
- loaf pan

1 **Preheat the oven** to 350°F (180°C), then lightly grease a 1lb (450g) loaf pan with butter. Pour the dried mixed fruit and cranberries into a bowl.

2 **Carefully pour** the warm tea over the fruit and stir everything together, making sure that all of the fruit is soaked in the tea.

3 **Pour in the honey** and beaten egg and gently mix together using a wooden spoon.

4 **Add the wheat flour,** baking powder, and pumpkin pie spice. Stir well to combine all the ingredients.

5 **Spoon the mixture** into the prepared pan and level the top. Bake for 20–25 minutes, or until cooked through.

20 mins, plus rising   20 mins   Serves 4

- 1½ cups lukewarm water
- 1 tsp salt
- 3 cups bread flour
- 1 tbsp olive oil

- ½ tsp sugar
- 1 tsp dried mixed herbs
- 7oz (200g) mozzarella cheese, grated

- 2 baking sheets
- sieve
- knife
- damp cloth
- wooden spoon
- rolling pin

Ingredients

- ½ tsp sugar
- 1 tsp active dry yeast

For the topping

- 1 cup passata
- 2 tbsp tomato paste

Equipment

- mixing bowl
- metal spoon
- saucepan

Put the sugar, yeast, and water in a bowl, mix, then leave for 5 minutes. In another bowl, sift the flour and salt, then add the oil and yeast mixture.

Stir with a knife to form a dough, then knead for 4–5 minutes. Place in a bowl, cover with a clean, damp cloth, and set in a warm place for 1 hour.

Meanwhile, make the pizza sauce. Place the passata, tomato paste, sugar, and herbs in a small pan and simmer gently for 5 minutes. Let cool.

Preheat the oven to 450°F (220°C). Using a floured hand, punch the dough to knock out the air, then knead it lightly on a floured surface.

Divide the dough in two, then roll out each half into a rectangle on the baking sheets. Spoon the pizza sauce over the top, then sprinkle with the cheese.

Add toppings of your choice to turn one into a meat pizza and one into a vegetarian pizza. Bake for 15 minutes until golden brown, before cutting each into squares.

Pizza Squares

There will certainly be a topping to please everyone in this recipe, which makes two large pizzas. You can add meat toppings to one pizza and vegetarian toppings to another.

Variation

Toppings like bell peppers, pineapple, ham, pepperoni, red onion, corn, and tomatoes are all tasty choices.

Four ways with pizzas

Try out these classic and new pizzas.

1

2

Tiny toms pizza

This is a classic combination of ingredients and flavors. Restaurants that serve pizza would have this at the top of their menus.

Ingredients
- pizza dough ball (from the recipe on page 280)
- 2–3 tbsp tomato paste or pizza sauce
- mozzarella ball
- 1 pint container grape tomatoes
- fresh basil leaves, to serve

Method
- Roll out your pizza dough on a floured surface into a circle that will fit your pizza pan.
- Spread the tomato paste over the pizza using the back of a spoon.
- Carefully cut the mozzarella ball into slices.
- Place the mozzarella slices onto the pizza (slightly overlapping) and scatter the grape tomatoes on the cheese.
- Bake the pizza in a preheated oven at 350°F (180°C) for 20 minutes.
- Garnish with a handful of torn, fresh basil leaves.

Hawaiian bites

These are a fun take on ham and pineapple pizza. They'll be snapped up quickly, so make sure you try one before they're all gone!

Ingredients
- pizza dough ball (from the recipe on page 280)
- 2–3 tbsp tomato paste or pizza sauce
- 8oz (227g) can pineapple chunks, drained
- 2½oz (60g) ham, cut into strips
- 5½oz (150g) mozzarella cheese, grated

Method
- On a floured surface, divide your pizza dough into 12 small balls. Flatten the balls so they form small circles about 3in (8cm) in diameter.
- Spread the tomato paste over the dough circles using the back of a spoon.
- Place a few pineapple pieces and strips of ham on each pizza.
- Sprinkle a little bit of grated mozzarella cheese over each pizza bite.
- Bake the pizzas in a preheated oven at 350°F (180°C) for 15 minutes.

Top this...

Check what you have in the pantry or fridge and make up your own toppings for your pizza. Here are ideas for ingredients you can use.

anchovies

baby spinach leaves

sliced bell peppers

pineapple

olives

chile peppers

pepperoni

cherry tomatoes

3

4

Mushroom madness

If you're a pizza fan, then this option is right up your alley. The mushrooms and mozzarella will melt in your mouth.

Ingredients

- 1 tbsp olive oil
- 4½oz (125g) mushrooms, sliced
- pizza dough ball (from the recipe on page 280)
- 2–3 tbsp tomato paste or pizza sauce
- mozzarella ball

Method

- Gently heat the oil in a frying pan and fry the mushrooms for 2 minutes.
- Roll out your pizza dough on a floured surface into a circle that will fit your pizza pan. Roll the dough as thinly as you can.
- Spread the tomato paste over the pizza using the back of a spoon.
- Cut the mozzarella ball into thin slices.
- Place the mozzarella and mushrooms onto the pizza.
- Bake the pizza in a preheated oven at 350°F (180°C) for 20 minutes.

Pizza pops

These fun lollipop-style pizzas are great for a party or a picnic. The combination of bell peppers and tomatoes is delicious.

Ingredients

- pizza dough (from the recipe on page 280)
- 2–3 tbsp tomato paste or pizza sauce
- 5½oz (150g) mozzarella cheese, grated
- half a yellow bell pepper, sliced
- 6 red cherry tomatoes, halved
- 6 yellow cherry tomatoes, halved

Special equipment

- white ovenproof sticks

Method

- Divide your pizza dough into 12 small balls. Flatten the balls so they form small circles that are approximately 3in (8cm) in diameter. Insert a stick into each uncooked dough circle.
- Spread the tomato paste over the dough circles using the back of a spoon.
- Decorate with grated mozzarella, bell peppers, and tomatoes.
- Bake the pizzas in a preheated oven at 350°F (180°C) for 15 minutes.

Mini burgers

These mini burgers are hard to beat. Make them for your family and friends. They'll soon be asking you when you're going to serve them again!

30 mins | 15 mins | Serves 6

Ingredients

- 9oz (250g) ground beef
- 1¾ oz (50g) Parmesan cheese, freshly grated
- ¼ cup fresh bread crumbs
- 1½ tbsp olive oil
- ½ garlic clove, crushed
- 1 tbsp onion, finely chopped
- 1 egg
- 1 tsp dried oregano
- olive oil, for frying

To Serve

- 16 mini hamburger buns
- 2 tomatoes, thinly sliced
- lettuce leaves

14 oz (400g) jar tomato sauce or salsa

Equipment

- large mixing bowl
- baking sheet
- frying pan
- spatula
- bread knife

1

Combine all the ingredients for the burgers in a bowl. Use your hands to mix everything together.

2

Form the mixture into balls and then flatten them. Chill the burgers in the fridge for 30 minutes. Wash your hands well.

3

Fry the burgers over medium heat. Make sure the meat is cooked through by putting a fork in and checking that the juice runs clear.

4

Carefully cut the buns in half. Fill each bun with a cooked hamburger, a tomato slice, a lettuce leaf, and tomato sauce.

Tip

You can decorate your mini burgers before serving them. Make flags out of colored strips of paper.

Cheese and pesto straws

Flavored with pesto and cheese, these light crisp straws are perfect for dipping.

Ingredients

- 1½ cups all-purpose flour
- 9 tbsp chilled butter, cut into small cubes
- 2oz (50g) Gruyère or Cheddar cheese, finely grated
- 2oz (50g) Parmesan cheese, finely grated
- 1 whole egg, plus 1 yolk
- 2 tbsp pesto sauce (either red or green)

25 mins   15 mins   Makes 30

Equipment

- sieve
- mixing bowl
- metal spoon
- rolling pin
- knife
- parchment paper
- baking sheet
- cooling rack

1

Preheat the oven to 350°F (180°C). Sift the flour into a bowl with a pinch of salt. Add the butter and rub in until it looks like fine bread crumbs.

2

Stir in 3oz (75g) of the cheeses. Beat together the egg and egg yolk and stir into the flour with the pesto sauce. Mix into a dough.

3

The mixture should be of the consistency where you can roll it into a ball.

4

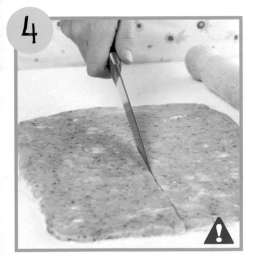

Roll out onto a lightly floured surface into a rectangle about 11 x 9in (28 x 23cm). Cut in half down the longest length, then cut each into about 15 straws.

5

Line a baking sheet with parchment paper. Transfer the straws to the baking sheet, leaving a gap between each.

6

Sprinkle over the remaining cheese and chill for 15 minutes. Bake for 12–15 minutes. Cool for 5 minutes on the sheet, then transfer to a cooling rack.

287

Tip

Keep your eye on the chips as they bake and remove them from the oven when they turn golden brown. Cool on a wire rack.

Use potatoes and carrots to make delicious oven-baked chips. Once you've made these, experiment with other vegetables, such as parsnips and beets.

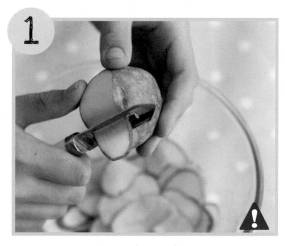

Preheat the oven to 350°F (180°C). For the potato chips, slice the potatoes using a peeler. Mix them with the oil, salt, pepper, and paprika, if using.

Line a baking sheet with parchment paper and arrange the potato slices in a single layer. Bake for 10 minutes, turn them over and bake for another 10 minutes.

For the carrot chips, use a vegetable peeler to slice the carrots thinly. Mix them with the oil, honey, salt, and pepper.

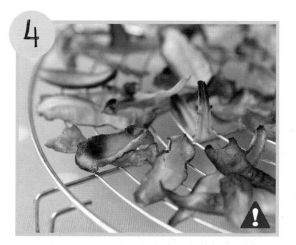

Line a baking sheet with parchment paper. Arrange the carrots in a single layer and bake for 10 minutes. Turn the chips over and bake for another 7–10 minutes.

20 mins   40 mins

Ingredients for the potato chips

- 2 medium potatoes
- 2 tsp sunflower oil
- salt and pepper
- 1–2 tsp paprika (optional)

For the carrot chips

- 2 medium carrots
- 2 tsp sunflower oil
- 2 tsp honey
- salt and pepper

Equipment

- vegetable peeler
- mixing bowl
- baking sheet
- parchment paper
- cooling rack

Vegetable platter

20 mins Serves 4

Ingredients

- 1 cucumber
- 2 celery ribs
- 1 red bell pepper, seeded
- 1 yellow bell pepper, seeded
- 2 carrots
- 4 baby gem lettuce leaves
- 8 cherry tomatoes
- 4 broccoli florets

Sour cream and chive dip

- ½ cup sour cream
- 3 tbsp fresh chives, chopped
- 2 tsp lemon juice

Yogurt and mint dip

- 1 cup plain yogurt
- ½ cucumber, grated
- 2 tsp dried mint

Equipment

- sharp knife
- cutting board
- 8 colorful cups and serving platter
- 2 small glass bowls
- 2 soup spoons

This healthy and colorful snack works well for any occasion or as a side dish to accompany a light meal.

Carefully slice the cucumber, celery ribs, bell peppers, and carrots into thin strips.

Put the vegetable sticks, lettuce leaves, cherry tomatoes, and broccoli florets in colorful cups. Arrange the cups on a platter and set aside.

Mix the sour cream, chives, and lemon juice in a small glass bowl. Pour into a colorful cup to serve.

In another small glass bowl, mix the plain yogurt, grated cucumber, and dried mint together. Taste and season with salt and pepper. Serve in a colorful cup.

Alternatives

There are plenty of other vegetables and dips you can add to a vegetable platter. Why not serve green beans and sugar snap peas and a tangy guacamole dip?

Dips and dippers

These dips are quick to make when you want something tasty to snack on while you're waiting for the main meal, for friends to arrive, or for the grill to heat up.

①

②

Guacamole

Use only ripe avocados. To check for ripeness, hold one in the palm of your hand and squeeze gently—it should give slightly.

Ingredients

This recipe is for 6 people. It takes 10 minutes to prepare.

· 2 ripe avocados
· juice of 1 lime
· ½ red onion, chopped
· 2 tomatoes, chopped
· 1 red chile, seeded and finely chopped
· 2 tbsp cilantro, chopped

Method

● Use a fork to mash the flesh of the avocados with the lime juice.

● Stir in the red onion, tomatoes, chile, and cilantro.

● Season with salt and freshly ground black pepper.

Tzatziki

When squeezing the cucumber in step 1, drain off as much water as you can, otherwise the tzatziki will be very runny.

Ingredients

This recipe is for 6 people. It takes 10 minutes to prepare.

· ½ a cucumber, peeled
· salt
· 1 garlic clove, finely chopped
· 1 cup Greek yogurt
· ½ a lemon
· 1 tbsp olive oil
· 1 tbsp fresh mint, chopped

Method

● Grate the peeled cucumber, sprinkle with a little salt, and squeeze in paper towels to remove excess water.

● Put the grated cucumber in a bowl and mix in the garlic clove, Greek yogurt, lemon juice, olive oil, and fresh mint.

Tastes great with...

These dips taste great with other recipes in the book. Dip potato wedges, chunks of pita bread, and vegetable sticks for a delicious snack.

vegetable chips

bell peppers

carrot sticks

bread sticks

3

Hummus

Hummus is very easy to make. It can be made with different ingredients, such as pine nuts, bell peppers, or, if you like spice, chiles.

Ingredients

This recipe is for 6 people. It takes 10 minutes to prepare.

· 14oz (400g) can chickpeas

· 2 garlic cloves, finely chopped

· juice of 1 lemon

· 2 tbsp tahini paste

· 3 tbsp olive oil

· pinch of paprika

· olive oil

· paprika

· 2 tbsp cilantro, chopped

Method

• Drain and rinse the can of chickpeas and pour them into a food processor.

• Add the chopped garlic, lemon juice, tahini paste, olive oil, and paprika. Blend until smooth.

• Serve with a drizzle of olive oil, a sprinkling of paprika, a few chickpeas, and the chopped cilantro.

4

Tomato salsa

A great crowd pleaser, tomato salsa is nutritious and yummy. Use the brightest red tomatoes to achieve the best taste.

Ingredients

This recipe is for 6 people. It takes 10 minutes to prepare.

· 6 tomatoes, coarsely chopped

· ½ an onion, chopped

· 1 garlic clove, finely chopped

· juice of ½ a lime

· 1 green chile pepper, seeded and finely chopped

· 2 tbsp olive oil

· 2 tbsp cilantro, chopped

Method

• Mix together the chopped tomatoes, onion, garlic clove, lime juice, chopped chile pepper, olive oil, and cilantro.

• Season with salt and freshly ground black pepper.

Very berry gelatin

These individual desserts are made using a mixture of frozen berries. Alternatively, you can pick just one type of berry, such as raspberry or blueberry.

5 mins 3 hrs setting Makes 4

Ingredients
- 5oz (135g) package raspberry or black currant flavored gelatin
- 150g (5½oz) mixed frozen berries

Equipment
- liquid measuring cup
- spoon
- gelatin molds

1

Place the gelatin in a liquid measuring cup and pour in 1 cup boiling water. Stir until the gelatin has dissolved.

2

Stir the fruit into the cup. Add cold water to make 2 cups, if necessary.

3

Spoon the mixture into one large gelatin mold or spread among four individual molds. Place in the fridge for about 3 hours, until set.

Tip

Make the recipe with frozen berries so the berries don't float to the top.

Variation

You can also serve your ice cream with chocolate sauce or chocolate chunks.

Ice cream

Pour, mix, and shake your way through this recipe to make delicious and refreshing ice cream. This frozen dessert doesn't have to go in the freezer!

12 mins | Serves 2

Ingredients
- ½ tbsp sugar
- ½ cup milk
- ½ cup heavy cream
- ¼ tsp pure vanilla extract
- 2lb (900g) ice cubes
- 7 tbsp coarse salt
- mixed berries (optional)

Equipment
- 2 resealable bags, 1 bigger than the other
- whisk
- mixing bowl
- wooden spoon
- clean dish towel

1

Whisk the sugar, milk, heavy cream, and vanilla in a bowl. Pour the mixture into a resealable bag, close it, and set aside.

2

Put the ice cubes into a large bowl and pour the coarse salt over the ice.

3

Fill a large resealable bag halfway full with ice cubes. Place the sealed bag of cream mixture into the bag of ice.

4

Fill the rest of the large bag with ice cubes and close it.

5

Wrap the large bag in a towel and shake for 10 minutes, or until the cream mixture has become solid. Serve immediately.

Lemonade ice pops

Keep cool on a hot summer day with the zingy taste of juicy lemon ice pops. Lemons add flavor to fish and salads as well.

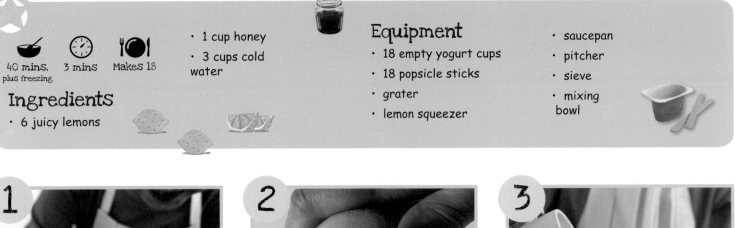

40 mins, plus freezing · 3 mins · Makes 18

- 1 cup honey
- 3 cups cold water

Ingredients
- 6 juicy lemons

Equipment
- 18 empty yogurt cups
- 18 popsicle sticks
- grater
- lemon squeezer
- saucepan
- pitcher
- sieve
- mixing bowl

1

Finely grate the zest from 3 of the lemons and place in a pan with the honey and 2 cups water. Bring to a boil, then remove from the heat.

2

Squeeze the juice from all of the lemons. Pour into a pitcher. This should give you about 1 cup of juice.

3

Strain the honey and lemon water through a sieve into a bowl. Pour in some of the lemon juice. Stir and taste. Add more juice until it tastes right.

4

Let the lemonade cool in the fridge. Add the rest of the water to dilute. Stir, then pour into 18 empty yogurt cups. Place in the freezer until partly set.

5

Push a popsicle stick into each cup. Return the cups to the freezer until the lemonade becomes completely solid.

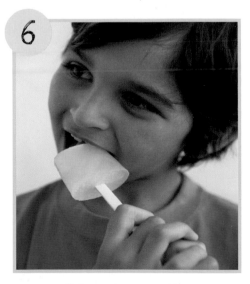

6

Crunch! Enjoy the cold juicy taste, but don't eat it too slowly—your ice pop will melt quickly on a warm day.

Index

Acknowledgments

Photography: Will Heap, Lisa Linder, Dave King, Howard Shooter, Craig Robertson; **Home economists:** Katherine Ibbs, Aya Nishimura, Paul Jackman, Kate Blinman, Katy Greenwood, Denise Smart; **Assistant home economists:** Lisa Harrison, Sarah Tildesley, Fergal Connolly; **Food stylists:** Suzie Harrison, Denise Smart, Annie Nichols, **Illustrations:** Takashi Mifune, Malting Partnership, Hennie Haworth, Rosie Scott; **Consultants:** Jill Bloomfield, Nicola Graimes, Denise Smart, Maggie Mayhew, Donald R. Franceschetti; **RHS consultant:** Simon Maughan; **Models:** Max Moore, Roberto Barney Allen, Fiona Lock, Peter Lock, Serena Patel, Christian Rivas-Lastic, Eva Rose Menzie, Ella Menzie, Omid Alavi, George Arnold, Alexander Whillock, Cherry Cameron, Sophia Zeynep, Christian Hannah, Solly, Fiona, Molly; **Recipe testing:** Jan Stevens; **Index:** Hilary Bird; **Garden care:** Capel Manor College.

About the authors

Jill Bloomfield is the creator of the cooking consulting company Picky Eaters. Originally a micro-business that provided hands-on children's cooking parties, Picky Eaters evolved as the "kids in the kitchen" trend caught fire.

Katherine Ibbs is an experienced home economist and food stylist. A believer in the importance of learning about cooking from an early age, she has taught cooking classes for kids and contributed to numerous children's cookbooks.

Nicola Graimes is an award-winning cookery and food writer. She is eager to show that eating well not only influences the health of our bodies and minds, but can also be delicious and fun.

Denise Smart has been a prolific recipe writer for the past 15 years. Her experience as a photographic home economist and food stylist has seen her work published nationally and internationally.